AF713753

The Psychology of Eyewitness Identification

Arguing for a need to modify investigatory and legal processes so that they align with the capabilities of witnesses and reflect the memorial and decision processes that inform recognition judgements, this book examines two radical alternative approaches to lineup-based recognition that do not require witnesses to identify a perpetrator: Non-categorical confidence and non-categorical similarity judgements.

Using empirical data, the authors explore the relationship between identification decisions, confidence judgements, and similarity judgements in lineup-based recognition tasks and reflect on whether similarity underpins more complex judgements of identity and confidence. They also examine the practical utility of confidence and similarity judgements and consider how such alternatives might be conceptualised in a legal context. This book draws on the areas of psychology and law to outline the key issues of identification and calls for a revision in how we think about, obtain, and present eyewitness evidence from lineups.

Prompting a consideration of new solutions and concepts to help witness errors become a problem of the past, *The Psychology of Eyewitness Identification* will be of great interest to students, scholars, and practitioners across the fields of criminal justice, psychology, and law, and particularly those with a focus on eyewitness identification.

Dominic T. Jordan is a Lecturer in Criminology at Edith Cowan University and a consultant researcher in the private sector. Dominic has previously held positions as a researcher within the Sellenger Centre for Research in Law, Justice, and Social Change, and as an officer of the Australian Government's National Anti-Corruption Commission. His research examines the role of human memory in investigative contexts, with a particular focus on eyewitness identification.

Adrian J. Scott is a Reader (Associate Professor) in Psychology at Goldsmiths, University of London, where he is Co-Director of the Forensic Psychology Unit and of an accredited MSc programme in Forensic

Psychology. Adrian is a chartered psychologist with associate fellow status within the British Psychological Society and has a broad interest in forensic psychology, specialising in the areas of investigative interviewing, eyewitness testimony, stalking, and image-based sexual abuse.

Donald M. Thomson is an Emeritus Professor of Psychology at Deakin University. During his career, Donald developed several postgraduate forensic psychology programmes in Australia, worked as a barrister at the Victorian Bar, and contributed to numerous professional bodies, law reform commissions, and advisory committees. He is a globally renowned expert in the areas of applied cognitive psychology, memory, recognition, and criminal law.

Routledge Frontiers of Criminal Justice

Cross-border Victims in Europe
Legal and Practical Barriers to Free Movement of Victims in Europe
Edited by Elżbieta Hryniewicz-Lach and Michael Kilchling

Legal Implications of Taser Use and Prone Position on Excited Delirium Subjects
Vidisha Barua Worley

Through the Distorted Lens
Constructing Truth and Reality with Legal Narratives
Fiona C. Hum

Youth Diversion
Exploring Criminal Justice Perspectives through An Australian Case Study
Estrella Pearce

Beyond Autoethnography
Lived Experience Criminology
Dwayne Antojado, Danica Darley, and Matthew Maycock

The Psychology of Eyewitness Identification
Exploring the Relationship Between Traditional and Alternative Approaches to Recognition
Dominic T. Jordan, Adrian J. Scott, and Donald M. Thomson

For more information about this series, please visit: www.routledge.com/Routledge-Frontiers-of-Criminal-Justice/book-series/RFCJ

The Psychology of Eyewitness Identification

Exploring the Relationship Between Traditional and Alternative Approaches to Recognition

Dominic T. Jordan, Adrian J. Scott and Donald M. Thomson

Routledge
Taylor & Francis Group
LONDON AND NEW YORK

First published 2026
by Routledge
4 Park Square, Milton Park, Abingdon, Oxon OX14 4RN

and by Routledge
605 Third Avenue, New York, NY 10158

Routledge is an imprint of the Taylor & Francis Group, an Informa business

© 2026 Dominic T. Jordan, Adrian J. Scott, and Donald M. Thomson

The right of Dominic T. Jordan, Adrian J. Scott, and Donald M. Thomson to be identified as authors of this work has been asserted in accordance with sections 77 and 78 of the Copyright, Designs and Patents Act 1988.

All rights reserved. No part of this book may be reprinted or reproduced or utilised in any form or by any electronic, mechanical, or other means, now known or hereafter invented, including photocopying and recording, or in any information storage or retrieval system, without permission in writing from the publishers.

For Product Safety Concerns and Information please contact our EU representative GPSR@taylorandfrancis.com. Taylor & Francis Verlag GmbH, Kaufingerstraße 24, 80331 München, Germany.

Trademark notice: Product or corporate names may be trademarks or registered trademarks, and are used only for identification and explanation without intent to infringe.

British Library Cataloguing-in-Publication Data
A catalogue record for this book is available from the British Library

ISBN: 978-1-032-94282-7 (hbk)
ISBN: 978-1-032-94286-5 (pbk)
ISBN: 978-1-003-56992-3 (ebk)

DOI: 10.4324/9781003569923

Typeset in Times New Roman
by SPi Technologies India Pvt Ltd (Straive)

Contents

Figures

Tables

Acknowledgements

The authors would like to thank Aimee Wrightson-Hester for her helpful comments and feedback on draft versions of the book, and Pamela Henry for her support throughout the duration of the research. The first author would also like to acknowledge the support of the Australian Government through an Australian Government Research Training Program Scholarship.

Data Availability Statement

The full dataset supporting the findings of this book is available from the corresponding author, D. T. Jordan, upon reasonable request. A subset of this data was previously published in Jordan et al. (2025) under a Creative Commons Attribution 4.0 International License and is publicly accessible via the Open Science Framework at https://doi.org/10.17605/OSF.IO/4XR6Z.

1 Introduction and Overview

In a criminal trial, there is no more compelling evidence than the identification of a suspect by a witness or witnesses to a crime (Leippe, 1995; Pozzulo & Dempsey, 2009). Unfortunately, a substantial body of evidence has shown that eyewitness identification is highly fallible and often mistaken (Clark et al., 2008; Horry et al., 2014; Steblay et al., 2011). Findings from both empirical and field research suggest that witnesses make identification errors in approximately 50% of lineups (Amendola & Wixted, 2015; Clark et al., 2008; Horry et al., 2014; Fitzgerald et al., 2015; Steblay et al., 2011; Valentine et al., 2003). Furthermore, real-world data show eyewitness identification errors have contributed to many of the known cases of wrongful conviction (Innocence Project, 2016, 2025; National Registry of Exonerations, 2025). These findings are particularly concerning, given the profound negative consequences of wrongful convictions. Not only is an innocent person punished, but a guilty person is not punished, and community trust in the criminal justice system is undermined (Clark, 2011; Lampinen et al., 2018).

More than half a century of empirical research has aimed to understand and improve eyewitness identification, yet mistaken identifications continue to contribute to costly errors during the investigatory and evidentiary stages of the criminal justice system. In most legal contexts, an identification is an assertion by a witness that they recognise a person in a lineup as the person they saw at the time of a criminal event (Australian Law Reform Commission [ALRC], 2006; *Jury Directions Act* 2015 s35 [Vic]). Thus, it is assumed that a witness, when presented with a lineup, can reliably determine whether a lineup member is the *same* person previously seen committing a crime. However, the capability of witnesses to make these judgements of sameness is the subject of much debate (ALRC, 2006; Levi & Jungman, 1995; Thomson, 1989; Zwartz et al., 2024). Although most eyewitness researchers appear to accept that witnesses can make judgements of this nature (albeit, often inaccurately), certain sections of the research community have challenged this assumption (Levi & Jungman, 1995; Navon, 1990; Thomson, 1986; Zwartz et al., 2024).

DOI: 10.4324/9781003569923-1

Recently, we argued that the notion of identification or sameness that is currently affixed to eyewitness evidence is flawed (Jordan et al., 2025; Zwartz et al., 2024). Specifically, we believe there are two main issues of identification: one psychological, the other legal (Zwartz et al., 2024). The *psychological issue* pertains to the fact that witnesses may lack the necessary information required to reliably identify a perpetrator presented as part of a lineup when encountered only briefly at the time of a criminal event (Jordan et al., 2025; Levi & Jungman, 1995; Thomson, 1982, 1989). This is because, in the absence of familiarity or prior knowledge of a perpetrator's identity, the primary source of information available to witnesses is the perceptual cues associated with their appearance (Levi & Jungman, 1995; Thomson, 1982, 1986); and appearances can be deceiving (Jordan et al., 2025). The *legal issue* pertains to the fact that the strength attributed to identification evidence far outweighs its probative value (i.e., evidentiary or legal proof; see Wells et al., 2006). Indeed, we argue that eyewitness evidence, when presented as direct evidence, has the potential to usurp or subsume the role of triers of fact (e.g., judge, jury; Thomson, 1982, 1989; Zwartz et al., 2024).

To maximise the value of eyewitness evidence and reduce the incidence of costly errors, there is a need to address these issues of identification, both psychological and legal. To address this gap effectively, we believe eyewitness researchers need to eschew the constraints of the enduring traditional identification approach and develop alternative approaches to recognition that currently exist outside the realm of what is considered reasonable or practicable (Jordan et al., 2025). Consistent with this belief, we and several other eyewitness researchers have sought to develop and test a range of alternative approaches for obtaining eyewitness evidence from lineups (e.g., Ayala et al., 2022; Brewer & Doyle, 2021; Gepshtein et al., 2020; Huang & Fitzgerald, 2023; Mu et al. 2017; Smith et al., 2023; Yilmaz et al., 2025; Zwartz et al., 2024). Two such alternatives, the non-categorical confidence approach (Brewer & Doyle, 2021; Brewer et al., 2020; Brewer et al., 2012; Bruer et al., 2017; Sauer et al., 2008; Sauer et al., 2012a, 2012b; Weber & Varga, 2012) and the non-categorical similarity approach (Jordan, 2021; Zwartz, 2016; Zwartz et al., 2024), position the eyewitness decision task as involving multiple match-based comparisons rather than a single categorical decision. That is, witnesses refrain from making an identification, and instead express judgements regarding how confident (or certain) they are that each member of a lineup is the perpetrator (i.e., confidence judgements), or how similar each lineup member is to their memory of a perpetrator (i.e., similarity judgements).

While initial assessments indicate that both confidence (e.g., Brewer et al., 2020; Sauer et al., 2008) and similarity (e.g., Jordan, 2021; Zwartz et al., 2024) judgements can facilitate recognition in lineup tasks by allowing witnesses to access diagnostic memorial information (i.e., match-to-memory), continued examination of non-categorical approaches and their use in lineups is required (Colloff et al., 2021; Sauer et al., 2019; Smith & Ayala, 2021). Indeed, there is still much to be learned regarding the confidence and similarity constructs and how they have been operationalised in lineup-based recognition contexts (Colloff et al., 2021; Dodson & Garrett, 2021; Jordan, 2021; Sauer et al., 2019; Smith & Ayala, 2021). For example, there is a need to further explore how confidence and similarity judgements are distributed within lineups and how these correspond with each other and identification decisions. Moreover, little attention has been afforded to how these judgements are elicited or influenced under varying conditions, such as when perpetrator appearance changes (Jordan, 2021; Jordan et al., 2025). Finally, there is a paucity of research examining whether confidence and similarity judgements can accurately discriminate or distinguish correct from incorrect responses in lineup-based recognition tasks, and if either approach can compete with, or outperform, the identification approach. In this book, we seek to address these gaps in the literature by developing a richer and more robust understanding of both traditional and alternative approaches (i.e., identification decisions, confidence judgements, and similarity judgements) to obtaining evidence from lineups. Specifically, it will address the following two research aims:

Aim 1: To explore the theoretical relationship between identification, confidence, and similarity in lineup-based recognition tasks.
Aim 2: To evaluate the practical utility of confidence and similarity judgements as alternatives to identification decisions in lineup-based recognition tasks.

To address these research aims, we investigate how responses obtained using the three recognition approaches compare and compete in lineup-based recognition tasks. First, we explore the correspondence between responses obtained using the identification, confidence, and similarity approaches. As part of this, we reflect on prior claims that similarity informs and underpins judgements of confidence and identity (Fitousi, 2024; Zwartz, 2016), and that confidence serves as a relatively direct proxy for similarity in lineup-based recognition tasks (Sauer et al., 2008). Second, we examine whether the two non-categorical approaches, and the information unique to them both, can be used to facilitate and improve accurate recognition when compared to the identification approach. Specifically, we consider whether the confidence and similarity approaches perform strongly enough to be considered viable alternatives to the identification approach in real-world contexts. Importantly, the empirical findings related to both aims will guide the discussion in Chapter 6 regarding how confidence and similarity judgements might be positioned to address the psychological and legal issues of identification.

Our research utilises data from 1,020 participants who each completed four lineups that involved: viewing a target person, completing a brief distractor task, and responding to a lineup. We also manipulated three variables of interest. The first was recognition approach, a between-participant manipulation, whereby participants made identification decisions with associated post-decisional confidence ratings (n = 350), confidence judgements (n = 314), or similarity judgements (n = 356). The second variable of interest was target appearance, a within-participant manipulation, where the targets' appearance changed or did not. The third and final variable of interest was target presence, another within-participant manipulation, where the target was present or absent from the lineup.

Book Structure

Throughout the remaining five chapters of this book, we seek to provide researchers and practitioners with valuable insights into what we consider to be key big picture issues associated with the psychology of eyewitness identification. The two alternative approaches we examine represent a significant departure from the traditional identification approach, and address what has been described as the "profound conservatism" of many research innovations in this area (Wells et al., 2006).

In Chapter 2, we review relevant psychological and legal literature, directly building on the key information presented in this chapter. Specifically, we seek to provide a foundational understanding of the three recognition approaches of interest by drawing on relevant psychological research and theory. We critically appraise the traditional identification approach while elaborating on the psychological and legal issues introduced in this chapter. We examine the role of confidence in recognition contexts, discuss the advent of the confidence approach, and consider the theoretical association between confidence and identity in lineup-based recognition tasks. We also discuss the importance of similarity in recognition contexts, acknowledge the current lack of scholarly knowledge regarding the similarity approach, and consider the theoretical association between similarity and identity in lineup-based recognition tasks.

In Chapter 3, we consider the role of appearance in recognition contexts and outline the methodological approach to our research. Notably, we highlight the importance of perpetrator appearance in recognition contexts and explain its relevance when examining the theoretical and practical utility of traditional and alternative approaches to obtaining eyewitness evidence from lineups. We also provide information regarding the research participants, design, materials, and procedure. We explain how the research presented in this book utilises data collected as part of the first author's PhD (Jordan, 2021), and how our methodological approach extends on the original work. Further methodological information regarding our general analytic approach will be threaded throughout the book.

In Chapter 4, we present the first set of empirical findings to address the first research aim: To explore the theoretical relationship between identity, confidence, and similarity in lineup-based recognition tasks. Specifically, we explore how the distribution of identification decisions, confidence judgements, and similarity judgements correspond within lineups; as well as how changes to target appearance between encoding and retrieval influence identification decisions (and post-decisional confidence ratings), confidence judgements, and similarity judgements across lineups. In this chapter, we relate the empirical findings to relevant literature and reflect on assumptions made in prior research regarding the three recognition approaches and the relationships they have with each other.

In Chapter 5, we present the second set of empirical findings to address the second research aim: To evaluate the practical utility of confidence and similarity judgements as alternatives to identification. Specifically, we examine the discrimination accuracy (discrimination) and reliability of identification decisions (and post-decisional confidence ratings), confidence judgements, and similarity judgements; and whether additional information unique to confidence and similarity judgements (i.e., discrepancy) can be used to enhance eyewitness discrimination. In this chapter, we relate the empirical findings to relevant literature and consider whether confidence and similarity judgements might be considered viable for use in applied settings.

In Chapter 6, we synthesise the main empirical findings of our research, discuss the implications for the psychological and legal issues of identification, and outline research limitations and directions for future research. In this chapter, we argue that identification decisions, confidence judgements, and similarity judgements access and rely on the same match-to-memory information. Although we acknowledge that non-categorical judgements are susceptible to the same errors as identification decisions, we believe they should better reflect the cognitive capabilities of witnesses. Further, we argue that if witness errors are to become a problem of the past, investigatory and evidentiary practice must align with witness capabilities, and the strength attributed to identification evidence must align with its probative value. Importantly, Chapter 6 does not seek to close the door on the issues of identification but rather serves as a launching pad for future debate and research.

Summary

In this chapter, we provided initial contextual information relating to eyewitness identification and the three recognition approaches of interest.

We introduced the main psychological and legal issues associated with the traditional identification approach, and described two alternative approaches to obtaining eyewitness evidence from lineups: confidence and similarity judgements. We described the aims and rationale for examining confidence and similarity judgements as alternatives to identification decisions and outlined the structure and content of subsequent chapters. In Chapter 2, we build on this foundational understanding by critically appraising the traditional identification approach and providing an in-depth examination of the confidence and similarity constructs in lineup-based recognition contexts.

References

Amendola, K. L., & Wixted, J. T. (2015). Comparing the diagnostic accuracy of suspect identifications made by actual eyewitnesses from simultaneous and sequential lineups in a randomised field trial. *Journal of Experimental Psychology*, *11*, 263–284. https://doi.org/10.1007/s11292-014-9219-2

Australian Law Reform Commission. (2006). *Identification evidence*. Retrieved from www.alrc.gov.au/publications

Ayala, N. T., Smith, A. M., & Ying, R. C. (2022). The rule-out procedure: Increasing the potential for police investigators to detect suspect innocence from eyewitness lineup procedures. *Journal of Applied Research in Memory and Cognition*, *11*(4), 489–499. https://doi.org/10.1037/mac0000018

Brewer, N., & Doyle, J. (2021). Changing the face of police lineups: Delivering more information from witnesses. *Journal of Applied Research in Memory and Cognition*, *10*(2), 180–195. https://doi.org/10.1016/j.jarmac.2020.12.004

Brewer, N., Weber, N., & Guerin, N. (2020). Police lineups of the future? *American Psychologist*, *75*(1), 76–91. https://doi.org/10.1037/amp0000465

Brewer, N., Weber, N., Wooton, D., & Lindsay, D. S. (2012). Identifying the bad guy in a lineup using confidence judgements under deadline pressure. *Psychological Science*, *23*(10), 1208–1214. https://doi.org/10.1177/0956797612441217

Bruer, K. C., Fitzgerald, R. J., Price, H. L., & Sauer, J. D. (2017). How sure are you that this is the man you saw? Child witnesses can use confidence judgments to identify a target. *Law and Human Behaviour*, *41*(6), 541–555. https://doi.org/10.1037/lhb0000260

Clark, S. E. (2011). Blackstone and the balance of eyewitness identification evidence. *Albany Law Review*, *74*(3), 1105. Retrieved from http://www.heinonline.org.ezproxy.ecu.edu.au/HOL/Page?public=false&handle=hein.journals/albany74&page=1105&collection=journals

Clark, S. E., Howell, R. T., & Davey, S. L. (2008). Regularities in eyewitness identification. *Law and Human Behaviour*, *32*(3), 187–218. https://doi.org/10.1007/s10979-006-9082-4

Colloff, M. F., Wilson, B. M., & Flowe, H. D. (2021). Legal system v. eyewitness: The jury is still out on who is better able to reduce eyewitness error (variance). *Journal of Applied Research in Memory and Cognition*, *10*(2), 200–204. https://doi.org/10.1016/j.jarmac.2021.04.001

Dodson, C. S., & Garrett, B. L. (2021). Can we get over IDs? *Journal of Applied Research in Memory and Cognition*, *10*(2), 212–214. https://doi.org/10.1016/j.jarmac.2021.03.008

Fitousi, D. (2024). A signal detection-based confidence-similarity model of face matching. *Psychological Review*, *131*(3), 625–663. https://doi.org/10.1037/rev0000435

Fitzgerald, R. J., Oriet, C., & Price, H. L. (2015). Suspect filler similarity in eyewitness lineups: A literature review and a novel methodology. *Law and Human Behaviour*, *39*(1), 62–74. https://doi.org/10.1037/lhb0000095

Gepshtein, S., Wang, Y., He, F., Diep, D., & Albright, T. D. (2020). A perceptual scaling approach to eyewitness identification. *Nature Communications*, *11*(1), 1–10. https://doi.org/10.1038/s41467-020-17194-5

Horry, R., Halford, P., Brewer, N., Milne, R., & Bull, R. (2014). Archival analysis of eyewitness identification test outcomes: What can they tell us about eyewitness memory? *Law and Human Behaviour*, *38*(1), 94–108. https://doi.org/10.1037/lhb0000060

Huang, C., & Fitzgerald, R. J. (2023, March 1–8). *An alternative approach to the rule-out lineup procedure* [Conference Session]. *American Psychology-Law Society Annual Conference*, Philadelphia, PA, United States. https://ap-ls.org/conferences/schedule.html

Innocence Project. (2016). *The cases*. Retrieved from http://www.innocenceproject.org/all-cases/#eyewitness-misidentification,exonerated-by-dna.

Innocence Project. (2025). *Eyewitness Misidentification*. Retrieved from https://innocenceproject.org/eyewitness-misidentification/

Jordan, D. T. (2021). *Identity: A crisis of confidence? Or is it resemblance? An exploration of the different approaches by which eyewitness evidence can be obtained from lineups*. [Doctoral thesis, Edith Cowan University]. Research Online Institutional Repository. https://ro.ecu.edu.au/theses/2449

Jordan, D. T., Scott, A. J., & Thomson, D. M. (2025). Appearances can be deceiving: How naturalistic changes to target appearance impact on lineup-based decision making. *Psychology, Crime & Law*, *31*(4), 1–28. https://doi.org/10.1080/1068316X.2023.2243001

Lampinen, J. M., Smith, A. M., & Wells, G. L. (2018). Four utilities in eyewitness identification practice: Dissociations between receiver operating characteristic analysis and expected utility analysis. *Law and Human Behavior*, *43*(1), 26–44. https://doi.org/10.1037/lhb0000309

Leippe, M. R. (1995). The case for expert testimony about eyewitness memory. *Psychology, Public Policy and Law*, *1*(4), 909–959. https://doi.org/10.1037/1076-8971.1.4.909

Levi, A. M., & Jungman, N. (1995). The police lineup: Basic weaknesses and radical solutions. *Criminal Justice and Behaviour*, *22*(4), 347–372. https://doi.org/10.1177/0093854895022004001

Mu, E., Chung, T., & Reed, L. (2017). Paradigm shift in criminal police lineups: Eyewitness identification as multi-criteria decision making. *International Journal of Production Economics*, *184*, 95–106. https://doi.org/10.1016/j.ijpe.2016.11.019

National Registry of Exonerations. (2025). *National Registry of Exonerations*. Retrieved from https://exonerationregistry.org/

Navon, D. (1990). How critical is the accuracy of an eyewitness's memory? Another look at the issue of lineup diagnosticity. *Journal of Applied Psychology*, *75*(5), 506–510. https://doi.org/10.1037/0021-9010.75.5.506

Pozzulo, J. D., & Dempsey, J. L. (2009). Witness factors and their influence on juror's perceptions and verdicts. *Criminal Justice and Behaviour*, *36*(9), 923–934. https://doi.org/10.1177/0093854809338450

Sauer, J. D., Brewer, N., & Weber, N. (2008). Multiple confidence estimates as indices of eyewitness memory. *Journal of Experimental Psychology*, *137*(3), 528–547. https://doi.org/10.1037/a0012712

Sauer, J. D., Brewer, N., & Weber, N. (2012b). Using confidence ratings to identify a target among foils. *Journal of Applied Research in Memory and Cognition*, *1*, 80–88. https://doi.org/10.1016/j.jarmac.2012.03.003

Sauer, J. D., Palmer, M., & Brewer, N. (2019). Eyewitness identification. In N. Brewer & A. Douglas (Eds.), *Psychological science and the law*. Guilford Press.

Sauer, J. D., Weber, N., & Brewer, N. (2012a). Using ecphoric confidence ratings to discriminate seen from unseen faces: The effects of retention interval and distinctiveness. *Psychonomic Bulletin and Review*, *19*, 490–498. https://doi.org/10.3758/s13423-012-0239-5

Smith, A. M., & Ayala, N. T. (2021). Do traditional lineups undermine the capacity for eyewitness memory to rule out innocent suspects? *Journal of Applied Research in Memory and Cognition*, *10*(2), 215–220. https://doi.org/10.1016/j.jarmac.2021.03.003

Smith, A. M., Ayala, N. T., & Ying, R. C. (2023). The rule out procedure: A signal-detection-informed approach to the collection of eyewitness identification evidence. *Psychology, Public Policy, and Law*, *29*(1), 19–31. https://doi.org/10.1037/law0000373

Steblay, N. K., Dysart, J. E., & Wells, G. L. (2011). Seventy-two tests of the sequential line-up superiority effect: A meta-analysis and policy discussion. *Psychology, Public Policy and Law*, *17*(1), 99–139. https://doi.org/10.1037/a0021650

Thomson, D. M. (1982). The realities of eyewitness identification. *Australian Journal of Forensic Sciences*, *14*, 150–157. https://doi.org/10.1080/00450618209411171

Thomson, D. M. (1986). Face recognition: More than a feeling of familiarity? In H. D. Ellis, M. A. Jeeves, F. Newcombe & A. Young (Eds.), *Aspects of Face Processing* (pp. 391–399). Elsevier.

Thomson, D. M. (1989). *Psychological fiction in the court room: And they did not live happily ever after. Unpublished Manuscript*. Monash University.

Valentine, T., Pickering, A., & Darling, S. (2003), Characteristics of eyewitness identification that predict the outcome of real lineups. *Applied Cognitive Psychology*, *17*, 969–993. https://doi.org/10.1002/acp.939

Weber, N., & Varga, M. (2012). Can a modified lineup improve the usefulness of confidence? *Journal of Applied Research in Memory and Cognition*, *1*, 152–157. https://doi.org/10.1016/j.jarmac.2012.06.007

Wells, G. L., Memon, A., & Penrod, S. D. (2006). Eyewitness evidence: Improving its probative value. *Psychological Science in the Public Interest*, *7*(2), 45–75. https://doi.org/10.1111/j.1529-1006.2006.00027.x

Yilmaz, A. S., Wilson, B. M., & Wixted, J. T. (2025). A Rate-them-all lineup procedure increases information and reduces discriminability. *Journal of Experimental Psychology: Applied*, *31*(1), 1–11. https://doi.org/10.1037/xap0000524

Zwartz, M. (2016). *Identity crisis in identification evidence: Similarity judgements as an alternative to identification decisions*. [Doctoral thesis, Deakin University]. Research Online Institutional Repository. http://dro.deakin.edu.au

Zwartz, M., Thomson, D. M., & Scott, A. J. (2024). Identity crisis in eyewitness testimony: Exploring visual similarity judgments as an alternative to identification decisions. *Criminal Law Journal*, *47*(2), 93–108.

2 Traditional and Alternative Approaches to Recognition

In this chapter, we provide a more in-depth overview of the three recognition approaches of interest (i.e., identification decisions, confidence judgements, and similarity judgements) by building on key information introduced in Chapter 1. Drawing upon established theory and research, we critique the traditional identification approach and explore the psychological and legal issues of identification. We also discuss the case for confidence and explore the advent of the non-categorical confidence approach. Finally, we discuss the significance of similarity and review existing knowledge relating to the non-categorical similarity approach.

Issues of Identification and the Traditional Identification Approach

As part of a criminal investigation, witnesses are often tasked with identifying an unknown perpetrator from a lineup (McGuire et al., 2015; Wells, 2014; Wells & Olson, 2003). In a typical lineup, witnesses are shown an array of people (between 6 and 12), in person, photograph, or video format, which comprises a suspect and known-innocent foils (Clark et al., 2010; Wells et al., 2006; Wells & Olson, 2003). Witnesses then make categorical identification decisions (identification decisions), whereby they select a member of the lineup as the perpetrator (Yes) or reject the lineup as not containing the perpetrator (No; Brewer et al., 2020; Davis & Loftus, 2012; Wells et al., 2020).

The accuracy of identification decisions varies as a function of the perpetrator's presence in a lineup. For example, the identification of the suspect represents a correct decision in perpetrator present lineups (i.e., correct suspect identification), where the suspect *is* the perpetrator, but an incorrect decision in perpetrator absent lineups (i.e., incorrect suspect identification), where the suspect *is not* the perpetrator. Conversely, the rejection of the lineup as not containing the perpetrator represents an incorrect decision in perpetrator present lineups (i.e., incorrect non-identification) but a correct

DOI: 10.4324/9781003569923-2

decision in perpetrator absent lineups (i.e., correct non-identification). The identification of a foil represents an incorrect decision, irrespective of the presence or absence of the perpetrator (i.e., incorrect foil identification; Clark et al., 2010; Wells et al., 2006; Wells & Olson, 2003).

Lineups that contain the perpetrator or an innocent suspect are both susceptible to error (Brewer et al., 2020; Wells et al., 2006; Wells & Olson, 2003). Arguably, incorrect suspect identifications have the highest degree of consequence (Clark, 2011; Lampinen et al., 2018) because they increase the likelihood of wrongful conviction (Albright, 2016; Clark, 2011; Wells, 1993). As mentioned in Chapter 1, the negative consequences associated with wrongful conviction are threefold. The first, and most damaging, is that an innocent person is punished (Clark, 2011; Lampinen et al., 2018). Punishing an innocent person not only has a severe negative impact on the individual (e.g., psychological trauma, loss of freedom, and criminalisation) but also poses a significant financial cost to society (i.e., cost of imprisonment and reparations; Clark, 2011; Halvorsen, 2004). The second consequence is that the guilty person is not apprehended. This poses problems to the criminal justice system, for not only has the perpetrator escaped justice, but they have also been afforded the opportunity to cause more harm to society through further criminality (Brewer et al., 2020). The third, and often overlooked consequence is that wrongful convictions can serve to undermine the degree of trust the public has in the criminal justice system. This lack of trust may create strong sentiments of public dissatisfaction towards other associated bodies, such as law enforcement and the government (Albright, 2016).

Although some eyewitness researchers have disputed whether incorrect suspect identifications are the sole or leading cause of wrongful conviction (Cutler et al., 1987), erroneous identification evidence has, to date, played a role in many of the known cases (Innocence Project, 2013, 2016). Of the 367 DNA exonerations to have occurred in the United States between 1989 and 2020, 65% of the original cases involved some form of mistaken identification evidence (Innocence Project, 2020). Furthermore, in as many as 50% of the original cases, the incorrect suspect identification was attributed as being the predominant factor considered by triers of fact in delivering a guilty verdict. Based on these outcomes, some researchers have argued that identification evidence provided by a witness represents the single greatest danger to an innocent suspect during a criminal trial (Brewer et al., 2020; Davis & Loftus, 2012; Levi & Jungman, 1995; Wells, 1993).

Researchers have sought to explain why identification decisions continue to contribute to costly errors during the investigatory and evidentiary stages of the criminal justice system process (Brewer & Wells, 2011; Wells et al., 2006). One explanation is that the existing framework for obtaining and presenting eyewitness evidence, namely, identification, is inadequate

(Brewer et al., 2020; Thomson, 1989). As discussed in Chapter 1, in many legal settings, an identification decision is considered "an assertion by a person to the effect that he or she recognises, a person or object *as the* person or object that he or she saw, heard or perceived" at the time of a criminal event (*Jury Directions Act* 2015 s35 [*Vic*]). It is assumed, therefore, that witnesses, when presented with a lineup, can make reliable determinations that a lineup member is the *same* person seen previously committing a crime (Steblay & Brooks, 2021). We have doubts regarding the veracity of this assumption and have instead argued, along with several other researchers and practitioners, that the notion of identification in both an investigatory and legal context is problematic (Australian Law Reform Commission [ALRC], 1985; Levi & Jungman, 1995; Navon, 1990; Thomson, 1989; Zwartz et al., 2024).

We believe there are two main issues associated with obtaining and presenting eyewitness evidence in terms of identification: One psychological, the other legal (Zwartz et al., 2024). The *psychological issue* pertains to the fact that witnesses may lack the necessary information required to reliably identify a perpetrator presented as part of a lineup, when encountered only briefly at the time of a criminal event (Levi & Jungman, 1995; Thomson, 1989). The third author, for example, argued that witnesses, when presented with a lineup, use the information available to them to make inferences regarding the *likely identity* of each lineup member (Thomson, 1989). According to theoretical accounts of recognition, such as signal detection theory, these inferences are based primarily on the perceptual or visual pattern of information available to a witness during the criminal event and lineup (Clark & Gronlund, 1996; Dunn, 2004; Malmberg, 2008; Wixted, 2007). Specifically, a witness compares the perceptual attributes associated with a person who is present (i.e., a lineup member) with their memory of the perceptual attributes of the perpetrator (Levi & Jungman, 1995; Thomson, 1989). This process of comparison generates a match-to-memory signal, often characterised as a subjective sense of similarity or feeling of familiarity (Malmberg, 2008; Tulving, 1981, 1983; Wixted, 2007). Signal detection accounts posit that a categorical identification decision in the context of a lineup-based recognition task results from the comparison of match-to-memory information against a pre-set internal threshold for responding, known as a decision criterion (Baranski & Petrusic, 2001; Clark, 2011; Sauer et al., 2008). When the match-to-memory associated with a specific lineup member exceeds a witness's decision criterion, that lineup member will be identified. Likewise, when the match-to-memory associated with a specific lineup member falls beneath a witness's decision criterion, that lineup member will not be identified.

We, and several other eyewitness researchers, have argued that using match-to-memory information to inform identification decisions can be misleading and almost certainly contributes to errors during the investigatory and evidentiary stages of the criminal justice system process (Brewer et al., 2020; Levi & Jungman, 1995; Thomson, 1989; Zwartz et al., 2024). Not only is match-to-memory information in the context of a lineup-based recognition task often weak (Semmler et al., 2018), it is negatively influenced by a wide range of factors outside the witness's and criminal justice system's control (e.g., poor viewing conditions and changes to perpetrator appearance; Charman et al., 2022; Giacona et al., 2021; Jordan et al., 2025; Lampinen et al., 2014; Lindsay et al., 2008; Smith et al., 2019). Further, while a lineup member may share many perceptual characteristics with a witness's memory of the perpetrator, thus generating a strong match-to-memory signal; this is not definitive evidence that they are the same person (Thomson, 1982). Conversely, while a lineup member may share few perceptual characteristics with a witness's memory of the perpetrator, thus generating a weak match-to-memory signal; this is not definitive evidence that they are not the same person (Jordan et al., 2025; Navon, 1990; Thomson, 1989). For this reason, we believe that a more transparent approach to obtaining eyewitness evidence from lineups, that better reflects witnesses' capabilities, would be one that does not frame the decision task in terms of identity (Jordan, 2021; Thomson, 1989; Zwartz et al., 2024).

Requiring witnesses to make identification decisions as part of a criminal investigation and then presenting them as such in court has implications for the criminal justice system. Indeed, if the process of recognition witnesses engage with is reliant on imprecise and subjective comparisons made on a match-to-memory continuum (Malmberg, 2008), then presenting eyewitness evidence in precise categorical terms in court is likely to be problematic. For this reason, Navon (1990) advised that evidence provided by a witness in a criminal trial should in no way act as a definitive marker of guilt. Despite this, current legal processes in many developed countries mandate that identification decisions obtained from lineups be presented as direct evidence (Albright, 2016; ALRC, 2006), which does not require presumptions or inferences from jurors because it provides a concrete representation of a criminal event that directly ties the suspect to the crime (Heller, 2006). In contrast, circumstantial evidence, which currently includes forensic and DNA evidence, does not directly implicate a suspect, thus rendering it a weaker form of evidence (Heller, 2006). This constitutes the main *legal issue* associated with eyewitness identification, namely, that the strength attributed to identification evidence outweighs its probative value (i.e., evidentiary, or legal proof; see Wells et al., 2006). For this reason, we suggest that eyewitness evidence, when presented as direct evidence, has the potential to usurp or subsume the role of triers of fact (Jordan, 2021; Thomson, 1982; Zwartz, 2016; Zwartz et al., 2024).

The role of a jury in criminal trials is to determine the facts of a case based on the evidence presented. In establishing a guilty verdict, a jury must establish beyond a reasonable doubt that the accused is the perpetrator of the crime committed. However, in presenting identification decisions from lineups as direct evidence, this responsibility is instead placed with a witness or witnesses to a crime. Triers of fact unsurprisingly find identification evidence to be highly compelling and difficult to dispute (Bruer & Pozzulo, 2014; Coyle & Thomson, 2014; Cutler et al., 1988; Leippe, 1995; Pozzulo & Dempsey, 2009; Pozzulo et al., 2006; Reardon & Fisher, 2011; Semmler et al., 2011). In fact, findings from empirical research indicate that mock jurors rarely question the veracity of identification evidence (Reardon & Fisher, 2011; Semmler et al., 2011), perhaps because they lack sufficient knowledge regarding the memorial and perceptual processes involved in making an identification decision from a lineup (Deffenbacher & Loftus, 1982; Houston et al., 2013; Leippe, 1995; Paterson et al., 2013). However, it is clear that in criminal trials, where a suspect is identified, the likelihood that triers of fact deliver a guilty verdict is high, regardless of whether the suspect is guilty or innocent (Pozzulo & Dempsey, 2009; Pozzulo et al., 2006). For this reason, it has been suggested that if the responsibility of "fact finder" is to be returned to the jury, eyewitness evidence needs to be presented in a transparent manner that reduces the strength it is currently attributed by law (ALRC, 2006).

We believe there is a need to address the issues of identification, both psychological and legal. The development of alternative frameworks or approaches for obtaining and presenting eyewitness evidence may be important in this regard. The appropriateness of any alternative approach is likely to depend on how well it captures match-to-memory information, and the ease and transparency with which this information can be interpreted in court. Guided by this rationale, researchers have sought to develop novel ideas for obtaining eyewitness evidence that are "radically different" to the traditional identification approach (see Ayala et al., 2022; Carlson et al., 2019a; Levi, 2006; Gepshtein et al., 2020; Huang & Fitzgerald, 2023; Price & Fitzgerald, 2015; Mu et al., 2017). We feel the most promising ideas are those which approach witness responses as involving multiple match-based comparisons rather than a single identification decision, such as the confidence (Brewer & Doyle, 2021) and similarity approaches (Zwartz et al., 2024).

Alternative Approaches to Identification

In this book, we aim to explore the theoretical relationship between identification, confidence, and similarity in lineup-based recognition tasks, and to evaluate the practical utility of confidence and similarity judgements as alternatives to identification decisions in lineup-based recognition tasks. To provide a robust understanding of the psychological constructs of interest, the following two sections outline the theoretical and empirical literature regarding the confidence and similarity approaches to recognition respectively.

The Case for Confidence

The association between confidence and recognition, particularly in the context of identification decisions, has been rigorously investigated by researchers over the last five decades (Borthwell et al., 1987; Brewer, 2006; Brewer & Wells, 2006, 2011; Cutler & Penrod, 1988; Palmer et al., 2013; Sauer et al., 2010; Sauerland et al., 2012; Sporer et al., 1995). Several researchers hypothesised that confidence may provide diagnostically useful information regarding the likely accuracy of identification decisions made from lineups (Brewer, 2006; Brewer & Wells, 2006; Juslin et al., 1996; Wixted et al., 2015; Wixted & Wells, 2017). Although initial findings from research evaluating the relationship between confidence and identification accuracy indicated that the association was weak and non-significant (Borthwell, et al., 1987; Sporer et al., 1995), more recent experiments adopting alternative measures (i.e., calibration analyses) have produced findings to suggest that confidence and identification decision accuracy are well calibrated and thus robustly associated (Brewer, 2006; Brewer & Wells, 2006, 2011; Juslin et al., 1996; Palmer et al., 2013; Sauer et al., 2010; Wixted et al., 2015; Wixted et al., 2016; Wixted & Wells, 2017). Findings of such a robust, if imperfect (Grabman et al., 2019; Martschuk et al., 2019; Smith & Leach, 2019; Wells & Quinlivan, 2009), association are now so well established that several eyewitness researchers have argued that confidence is the most important factor in determining the reliability of identification decisions (Semmler et al., 2018; Wells et al., 2020; Wixted et al., 2015; Wixted et al., 2016; Wixted & Wells, 2017).

Perhaps one reason that confidence has such intuitive appeal to eyewitness researchers is that empirical evidence, which supports an association between confidence and identification decision accuracy, has a strong theoretical basis (Baranski & Petrusic, 2001; Petrusic & Baranski, 2003; Sauer et al., 2008; Sauer et al., 2012a; Smith & Leach, 2019; Van Zandt, 2000; Yeung & Summerfield, 2012). Many theories of confidence processing (e.g., decisional and post-decisional locus theories) posit that confidence and decision making rely on the same information in memory, and thus confidence and identification are intrinsically related (Sauer et al., 2008; Sauer & Brewer, 2015; Van Zandt, 2000).

Proponents of the decisional locus account argue that in making an identification decision, witnesses make an internal comparison between lineup members and a memorial representation of the perpetrator witnessed during a crime. Confidence, within a decisional locus framework, reportedly indexes match-to-memory signal strength (Dobolyi & Dodson, 2013; Leippe et al., 2009) or the difference between match-to-memory signal strength and a witness's decision criterion (Brewer & Wells, 2006, 2011; Sauer & Brewer, 2015; Wixted et al., 2015). Regardless of which interpretation is favoured, for a positive identification (e.g., correct target identifications, and incorrect replacement and foil identifications), confidence may provide a relatively direct measure of the degree to which a present stimulus and memorial representation are similar (Sauer et al., 2008; Seelau, 1995). Further, for a non-identification, confidence may provide a measure of the degree to which a present stimulus and a memorial representation are dissimilar (Fitousi, 2024; Horry & Brewer, 2016; Jordan et al., 2025), though this relationship is less clear (see Seale-Carlisle, 2024; Smith et al., 2023).

Post-decisional locus theories differ somewhat from decisional locus theories; however, they also produce evidence in favour of a confidence-accuracy relationship. Unlike decisional locus theories, post-decisional locus theories suggest that confidence is established after a decision has been made (Baranski & Petrusic, 2001; Petrusic & Baranski, 2003; Van Zandt, 2000). According to post-decisional theories, the process of comparison that occurs between a physical stimulus and a memorial representation will produce evidence in support of two response options: That the physical stimulus and memorial representation are the same, or that the physical stimulus and memorial representation are different. Evidence in support of each response option is accumulated and stored separately in memory. Once the accumulated evidence for one response option crosses a witness's decision criterion, a decision in favour of that response option is made (i.e., an identification or a rejection; Baranski & Petrusic, 2001; Sauer et al., 2008; Sauer & Brewer, 2015). Vickers (1979) suggests that confidence is an index of the difference that exists between evidence in the two accumulated stores. Therefore, if there is a large degree of difference between the accumulated evidence, confidence will be high, but if only a small degree of difference exists between the accumulated evidence, confidence will be low.

Non-Categorical Confidence Judgements

Building upon the idea that confidence and accuracy in recognition are associated, a body of literature has proposed that non-categorical confidence judgements may be operationalised in place of identification decisions for obtaining eyewitness evidence from lineups (Brewer & Doyle, 2021; Brewer et al., 2012, 2020; Sauer et al., 2008, 2012a, 2012b; Weber & Varga, 2012). In a departure from the traditional identification approach, Brewer, Sauer, and colleagues developed the confidence approach whereby witnesses express judgements, on a continuous scale, regarding how certain they are that each member of a lineup is the perpetrator (i.e., witnesses do not make a categorical decision). Proponents have suggested that obtaining confidence judgements in place of a categorical identification decision (with or without an associated post-decisional confidence rating) is advantageous for two main reasons. First, confidence may produce a better assessment of a face's match-to-memory than a categorical identification decision (Brewer et al., 2020; Sauer et al., 2008). Second, the influence of non-memorial factors on witnesses' decision criteria (e.g., administrative pressures and facial ambiguity amongst lineup members; Wells, 1993) may be reduced (Sauer et al. 2012a) because witnesses are not required to make explicit decisions (i.e., Yes, that is the perpetrator; No, the perpetrator is not present).

In their initial examination of confidence judgements, Sauer et al. (2008) compared the accuracy of confidence judgements with identification decisions. Participants were asked to provide judgements on an 11-point decile scale (0–100%) indicating their confidence that each member of a lineup was a previously seen target (Sauer et al., 2008). To establish the accuracy of these judgements, patterns of confidence were converted into the equivalent of a categorical decision. For this purpose, a set of classification algorithms was developed, which allowed the authors to determine which member of a given lineup elicited the strongest memory signal, and whether the strength of that signal was enough to generate the equivalent of an identification decision. As part of this process, patterns of confidence judgements were collapsed to form a single value proposed to index recognition (index value; see Sauer et al., 2008). A separate critical value was then calculated using a statistical optimisation procedure, which served as a type of artificial criterion threshold (fit ratio; see Koriat & Goldsmith, 1996). Any index value that exceeded the optimised critical value was treated as a positive identification, and any value that fell below the critical value was treated as a non-identification. Optimised critical values were selected on the basis that they maximised the likelihood of correct decisions (i.e., correct confidence classifications; Sauer et al., 2008).

Sauer et al. (2008) found that confidence judgements compared favourably with the accuracy of identification decisions across four experimental studies. Some small advantages in accuracy were observed in target-present lineups when participants made confidence judgements compared with identification decisions from lineups. For example, in the third and fourth experiments, the proportion of correct confidence classifications was significantly higher than the proportion of correct identification decisions. More substantial advantages in accuracy were observed in target-absent lineups, whereby confidence judgements across all four experiments produced significantly higher proportions of correct responses than identification decisions. Although exploratory in nature, Sauer et al. concluded that these findings supported their hypothesis; namely, that confidence can act as a sensitive index of match-to-memory signal strength.

Similar findings have been observed across a range of other testing conditions, including when mini-lineup and face-recognition paradigms were used (Sauer et al., 2012a; Weber & Varga, 2012), when the retention interval was increased between encoding and retrieval (Sauer et al., 2012a), when judgements were recorded within a set time frame (Brewer et al., 2012), and among child witnesses (Bruer et al., 2017). Indeed, this body of literature has consistently shown that confidence judgements can be effective and may yield more accurate responses than identification decisions. It is perhaps unsurprising, then, that some proponents have suggested that avoiding the use of the traditional identification approach may reflect best practice for obtaining accurate witness decisions (Sauer & Brewer, 2015). Brewer, Sauer, and colleagues have even suggested that a process whereby witnesses make multiple non-categorical judgements rather than single categorical decisions may represent the "future" of lineups used in real-world investigations (Brewer & Doyle, 2021; Brewer et al., 2020; Sauer et al., 2012b; Sauer & Brewer, 2015).

Although some promising outcomes have been associated with confidence judgements, conclusions regarding the practical utility of confidence must be approached with caution (Colloff et al., 2021; Dodson & Garrett, 2021; Fisher, 2021; Jordan, 2021; Newirth, 2021; Rossmo, 2021; Steblay & Brooks, 2021). Indeed, there are several practical and methodological limitations associated with existing research on confidence judgements. For example, most of the published literature examining confidence judgements has replicated Sauer et al.'s (2008) approach to classifying data (see Brewer et al., 2020; Yilmaz et al., 2025 for exceptions). That is, they converted patterns of confidence into the equivalent of a categorical decision by using optimised critical values. Optimised critical values were selected on the basis that they maximised response accuracy, potentially inflating the proportion of correct responses observed in these experiments. Weber and Varga (2012) proposed that more conservative critical values can be established, specifically values which minimise the difference between the observed and estimated proportion of positive classifications. However, this does not address a potentially more problematic limitation of this approach; namely, that classification algorithms cannot be used to calculate the veracity of a confidence judgement (or pattern of judgements) made by a single witness. Indeed, Brewer et al. (2012) readily conceded that "it is impossible to calculate classification criterion [critical values] on a case-by-case basis" (p. 82). This conclusion suggests that the algorithms developed by Sauer et al. have limited practical applicability.

More recently, Brewer et al. (2020) sought to address some of the limitations associated with Sauer et al.'s (2008) classification algorithms. Specifically, Brewer et al. adopted hierarchical Bayesian parameter estimation to calculate posterior probabilities of guilt (i.e., in a manner akin to calibration or confidence-accuracy characteristic analyses, where probability of guilt is plotted as a function of the numerical value of confidence; see Brewer & Wells, 2006; Juslin et al., 1996) for four different maximum confidence judgements: target or target replacement (replacement), unique max, foil unique max, target or replacement shared max, and foil shared max. For context, max judgements describe a process of classification whereby lineup members are categorised based on whether they received the judgement with the highest numerical value for a given lineup and whether this was shared with any other lineup member(s). This method, which does not involve calculating optimised critical values, represents a departure from how non-categorical evidence obtained from lineups has been analysed in previous research (e.g., Brewer et al., 2012; Sauer et al., 2008; Sauer et al., 2012a; Weber & Varga, 2012). Instead, the authors used this method to provide a measure of "reliability" (see Colloff et al., 2021), and indicate how well max confidence judgements predict the probability that a member of the lineup was the target or replacement.

Findings from Brewer et al. (2020) were mostly consistent with previous research. Indeed, across six experiments, they found that the proportion of correct max confidence judgements was significantly higher than the proportion of correct identifications. In addition, when a target or replacement received the max confidence judgement in a lineup trial, the probability of "guilt" (i.e., the probability that the judgement occurred in a target-present lineup) increased considerably as the numerical size of the judgement increased. That is, max judgements made with high confidence were often accurate. Conversely, when a target or replacement did not receive the max confidence judgement in a lineup, the probability of "innocence" (i.e., the probability the judgement occurred in a target-absent lineup) was much higher. Interestingly, the authors also observed that the probability of guilt increased monotonically as a function of the difference between the max and next highest judgement in a given lineup (i.e., discrepancy). Notably, in lineups where there was a high discrepancy between the max and next highest judgement (i.e., one lineup member stood out), there was a high probability that the lineup member who received the max judgement was the target. Based on these findings, Brewer et al. concluded that confidence judgements offer a relatively sensitive index of match-to-memory and can provide additional diagnostic information, relative to identification decisions.

As mentioned previously, the advancement of an approach that does not require participants to make identification decisions represents something radically different to the traditional identification approach. Initial findings regarding confidence judgements have been promising, with Brewer, Sauer, and colleagues suggesting that they may offer a viable applied alternative to identification decisions (Brewer & Doyle, 2021;

Sauer & Brewer, 2015; Sauer et al., 2019). While some researchers have argued that this conclusion is somewhat premature (see Colloff et al., 2021; Dodson & Garrett, 2021; Newirth, 2021; Rossmo, 2021; Smith & Ayala, 2021; Steblay & Brooks, 2021), the fact that confidence judgements have been utilised effectively in several experimental studies provides tentative evidence to suggest that memory-based information from lineups can be expressed and obtained in terms other than identity. Despite this, we believe there are still several unresolved questions regarding the theoretical and practical utility of confidence judgements in lineup-based recognition tasks (Jordan, 2021).

Regarding the theoretical utility of confidence judgements, one point which still requires careful consideration is whether confidence as a construct offers the most appropriate or transparent expression of memorial information available to eyewitness researchers and criminal justice system stakeholders. In explaining this point, it is important to acknowledge that memory theorists have generally agreed that match-to-memory exists on a familiarity-type continuum, informed by an individual's subjective interpretation of similarity (Thomson, 1986; Tulving, 1981, 1983; Wixted, 2007). It seems counterintuitive, therefore, that a potential proxy, confidence, would be chosen to index match-to-memory signal strength in place of similarity. Researchers may have favoured confidence because the association between confidence and decision making has a strong theoretical basis, which is empirically well-established (Brewer, 2006; Brewer & Wells, 2006; Juslin et al., 1996; Wixted et al., 2015; Wixted & Wells, 2017). Alternatively, confidence might have been operationalised in place of similarity because confidence judgements and scales of confidence are a commonly utilised feature in empirical research, where similarity is not (Brewer, 2006). Zwartz (2016) makes an important point, however, in suggesting that using confidence in place of similarity may result in a less direct and transparent measure of match-to-memory information. In addition, Kantner and Dobbins (2019) advised that caution be used in presenting confidence as a pure measure of perceptual or evidence strength information in recognition contexts. Data from several studies have demonstrated that confidence, contrary to some existing claims, is heavily influenced by both memorial and non-memorial factors (Kantner & Lindsay, 2012; Selmeczy & Dobbins, 2013). As such, it seems likely that confidence is the product of many conflicting sources of information, including feelings of familiarity, deductive reasoning, and individual differences (Colloff et al., 2021; Dodson & Garrett, 2021).

Regarding the practical utility of confidence judgements, it remains unclear whether they can outperform identification decisions on the accuracy metric believed to be most important to policymakers: discrimination (Colloff et al., 2021). In the context of recognition, discrimination typically refers to a witness's capacity to accurately distinguish between targets (in target-present lineups) and replacements (in target-absent lineups; Mickes et al., 2012; Colloff et al., 2021). As outlined throughout this chapter, much of the existing research on confidence judgements has focused on comparing the proportion of correct responses in target-present and target-absent lineups independently (Brewer et al., 2012; Sauer et al., 2008, 2012b; Weber & Varga, 2012), or more recently, the reliability of max judgements made with varying levels of confidence or discrepancy (i.e., probability of guilt; Brewer et al., 2020). Several researchers have recently argued, however, that alternative approaches to lineup-based recognition must demonstrate consistent and substantial improvements in discrimination relative to identification decisions, if they are ever to be considered viable in applied settings (Colloff et al., 2021; Dodson & Garrett, 2021; Smith & Ayala, 2021; Yilmaz et al., 2025). The limited body of literature directly comparing the discrimination of max confidence judgements and identification decisions has produced mixed results. For example, some research has reported superior discrimination for confidence judgements (Sauer et al., 2012a; Smith & Ayala, 2021), where others have reported superior discrimination for identification decisions (Yilmaz et al., 2025, Experiment 2), or comparable performance (Yilmaz et al., 2025, Experiment 1). Due to these inconsistencies, it is difficult to draw any firm conclusions regarding the practical utility of confidence judgements and their potential for use in applied settings. As such, it is important to continue exploring whether confidence judgements can facilitate improvements in discrimination relative to traditional (i.e., identification decisions and post-decisional confidence ratings; Smith & Ayala, 2021) and other alternative (e.g., similarity judgements; Jordan, 2021) approaches to lineup-based recognition. An important aspect of this research is to explore how, or if, the additional information obtained from non-categorical judgements (e.g., discrepancy) can facilitate improvements in the accuracy of responses in lineup-based recognition tasks.

The Significance of Similarity

Similarity, much like confidence, has a strong theoretical association with recognition and is an essential component of many human cognitive tasks (Hiatt & Trafton, 2017; Larkey & Markman, 2005; Medin et al., 1993; Tversky, 1977). Theoretical models of similarity suggest that it is a *process* that involves making match-based comparisons between the properties or features of a set of objects (Medin et al., 1993; Ross, 2008; Tversky, 1977; Tversky & Gati, 1982). The degree to which objects are adjudged to be similar is determined by how closely the features of one object are perceived by the observer to "match" the features of another object. Conversely, the degree to which objects are adjudged to be dissimilar is determined by how the features of one object are perceived by the observer to "mismatch" or deviate from the features of another object (Medin et al., 1990, 1993; Tversky, 1977). Some researchers have theorised that the weight ascribed to specific features in determining the degree of match varies and is dependent upon which features are considered more diagnostically relevant at the time of comparison (Kaplan & Medin, 1997; Tversky, 1977).

Theoretical models of similarity processing point to an intuitive association between similarity and recognition (Kaplan & Medin, 1997; Markman & Medin, 1995; Medin et al., 1995). Indeed, several researchers have suggested that recognition decisions may constitute similarity judgements fitted to a categorical outcome (Kaplan & Medin, 1997; Markman & Medin, 1995). In explaining this point, consider that similarity refers to a *match-based comparison process*, while recognition refers to a *decision process* which relies on perceptual or memorial information to form match-based comparisons between objects. Of interest to decision theorists has been establishing the point at which objects are considered similar enough to be adjudged the same. Osgood (1949), for example, proposed that similar objects may be perceived as being the same if they exceed a certain threshold of similarity. Specifically, it was suggested that comparison objects will be adjudged to be the same at the point of non-discrimination; that is, the point at which two objects are similar enough that they cannot be distinguished.

Several theories of decision making, such as signal detection theory, offer an alternative and slightly more nuanced conceptualisation. These theories suggest that similarity does not act as the threshold informing recognition decisions; rather, similarity acts as the evidence on which recognition decisions are based. Although a subtle distinction, these theoretical accounts posit that an object is likely to be recognised when the quantity of similarity between objects is high enough to exceed an individual's decision criterion. Conversely, an object is likely to be rejected when the quantity of similarity between objects is low and fails to exceed an individual's decision criterion (Baranski & Petrusic, 2001; Fitousi, 2024).

Similarity processing and decision making theories infer that similarity judgements may underpin more complex recognition decisions. In conceptualising the theoretical relationship between similarity and recognition, however, it is important to distinguish between two processes, namely, ecphoric and perceptual similarity (Tulving, 1981, 1983). Ecphoric similarity involves the comparison of one or more present objects with an object stored in memory. Ecphoric similarity can be categorised as the degree to which one or more present objects match the properties of a previously studied object stored in and retrieved from memory (Tulving, 1981). Perceptual similarity, by comparison, involves the comparison of multiple present objects and can be characterised as the degree to which two or more objects in a set share or do not share properties.

In lineup-based recognition tasks, both ecphoric and perceptual similarity can influence decision making. For example, participants' judgements of ecphoric similarity inform how similar they perceive lineup members to be to their memory of a target; referred to by many eyewitness researchers as match-to-memory signal strength (Charman & Wells, 2007). Ecphoric similarity may be high when a lineup member resembles a person previously seen, resulting in both correct and incorrect identifications. Conversely, ecphoric similarity may be low when a lineup member does not resemble a person previously seen, resulting in incorrect and correct non-identifications. Participants' judgements of perceptual similarity, by contrast, inform how similar they perceive lineup members to be to each other. High perceptual similarity between lineup members may increase the difficulty participants have in discriminating between faces, which, in turn, makes decision making more challenging. The opposite is often true when high perceptual dissimilarity is observed within a lineup. Further complicating the role of similarity in lineup-based recognition tasks are the interactions which can occur between ecphoric and perceptual similarity.

For the most part, research on similarity in lineup-based recognition contexts has almost exclusively focused on perceptual similarity. Specifically, this body of literature has examined how the selection of foils and foil similarity to a target influence identification accuracy (Carlson et al., 2019b; Clark & Godfrey, 2009; Fitzgerald et al., 2013; Fitzgerald et al., 2015; Horry & Brewer, 2016; Shen et al., 2024; Tredoux, 2002). Historically referred to in terms of lineup fairness, this body of literature has produced mixed findings (Malpass et al., 2007; Ross, 2008). However, one relatively consistent finding is that as the perceptual similarity between the target, replacement, and foils increases, the accuracy of identification decisions decreases (Carlson et al., 2019b; Fitzgerald et al., 2015; Malpass & Lindsay, 1999; Tredoux, 2002). Ecphoric similarity in lineup-based recognition tasks has received comparatively less empirical attention. Perhaps one reason for this is that ecphoric similarity is reliant on the unique episodic experiences of individual participants and thus is difficult to manipulate or measure. Despite this, several researchers have discussed how ecphoric similarity might be examined and operationalised in a lineup-based recognition context (Leippe & Wells, 1995; Levi & Jungman, 1995; Navon, 1990; Thomson, 1989).

Navon (1990) described the relationship between identification and ecphoric similarity by suggesting that identification decisions represent the mechanism by which witnesses convey to a court that a suspect in a criminal investigation resembles their memory of a perpetrator. Navon, who it should be noted was not advocating for changes to the acquisition and presentation of eyewitness evidence, nevertheless seemed to argue that identification decisions are not true judgements of identity. Navon's argument, much like our own, is that when presented with a lineup, witnesses do not identify a perpetrator by recognising that they are the same person previously seen committing a crime. Rather, witnesses consider the similarity between each lineup member and a memorial representation of the perpetrator and make a categorical decision regarding the *likely identity* of the perpetrator based on this information (Levi & Jungman, 1995; Mu et al., 2017; Navon, 1990; Thomson, 1989).

Consistent with the argument presented by Navon (1990), Levi and Jungman (1995) proposed that witnesses are not capable of making reliable identification decisions and so instead make choices based on some internal scale of similarity when presented with a lineup-based recognition task. Unlike Navon, however, Levi and Jungman suggested that changes might be made in terms of obtaining and presenting eyewitness evidence. The authors discussed a hypothetical lineup procedure that would require witnesses to view a large photographic lineup (with a nominal size greater than 100) and make multiple "partial identifications" expressed in terms of resemblance (i.e., witnesses might be asked to select lineup members that resembled the person they saw committing the crime).

It is important to note here that resemblance and similarity are synonymous constructs in the context of this book. Consider that the definition of resemblance; "point of likeness: similarity" and similarity; "the quality or state of being similar: resemblance" both reference the other (Merriam Webster, 2025; Oxford Shorter Dictionary, 2007). Hiatt and Trafton, (2017) further suggested that resemblance could be defined as the degree to which stimuli are perceived to be similar. To date, some researchers appear to have favoured the term similarity (Sauer et al., 2012a; Tredoux, 2002; Zwartz et al., 2024) while others have favoured the term resemblance (Leippe & Wells, 1995; Levi & Jungman, 1995; Navon, 1990; Thomson, 1989). One explanation for this variation is that the identification decision process might be underpinned by judgements of ecphoric similarity; however, legal doctrine on eyewitness evidence appears to have adopted the term resemblance (i.e., evidence of resemblance). Therefore, research focused on memory-based decision tasks may favour similarity, whereas research concerned with the implications of inaccurate eyewitness testimony and how it is presented in court may favour resemblance.

Non-Categorical Similarity Judgements

It appears certain sectors of the research community support the notion that identification decisions may constitute little more than ecphoric similarity judgements, and that such judgements may be best presented in terms of resemblance (Levi & Jungman, 1995; Navon, 1990; Thomson, 1989). However, even researchers who have argued that similarity may form the basis of identification decisions have mostly neglected the construct as a mechanism for obtaining eyewitness evidence. In fact, there has been a paucity of research which has sought to operationalise ecphoric similarity as a construct for obtaining eyewitness evidence from lineups (Zwartz et al., 2024).

As discussed in this chapter, the development of the non-categorical confidence approach has seen some researchers claim that confidence may provide a relatively sensitive index of ecphoric similarity (e.g., Sauer et al., 2012a). However, we and several other researchers believe that inferring similarity from confidence may be problematic for two main reasons (Jordan, 2021; Seelau, 1995; Zwartz et al., 2024). First, although confidence has a robust relationship with decision accuracy, this relationship remains imperfect (Grabman, et al., 2019; Martschuk et al., 2019; Sauer et al., 2019; Wells & Quinlivan, 2009; Wixted & Wells, 2017) and has been used to indicate that confidence can be informed and influenced by non-memorial factors not associated with evidence strength (Colloff et al., 2021; Kantner & Dobbins, 2019; Steblay & Brooks, 2021; Steblay & Wells, 2020). Second, if similarity is synonymous with, or serves as the basis on which match-to-memory is established, using a proxy, confidence may provide a less transparent and direct measure (Seelau, 1995; Zwartz, 2016). As Seelau (1995) explained, if confidence is supposed to index the degree to which an identified lineup member is similar to a witness's memory of a perpetrator, then directly asking a witness to make a judgement of similarity should provide more insightful information regarding match-to-memory signal strength.

A small number of empirical studies have sought to explore the role ecphoric similarity might play in the decision making process (Carlson et al., 2019a; Charman & Wells, 2007, 2012; Huang & Fitzgerald, 2023; Seelau, 1995). However, to the best of our knowledge, only one published study has looked at operationalising similarity judgements in place of identification decisions in lineup-based recognition tasks (Zwartz et al., 2024). In this exploratory research, members of our research team examined whether ecphoric similarity ratings (i.e., similarity judgements) obtained from lineups might offer a viable method for obtaining and presenting eyewitness evidence in court (Zwartz et al., 2024). To examine this, participants were required to either adjudge how similar each lineup member was to their memory of a target (similarity condition) or make an identification decision (identification condition). For the purposes of analysis, the lineup member who received the highest value similarity judgement (i.e., the max judgement) was treated as being "identified".

In contrast with research which has examined confidence judgements (e.g., Sauer et al., 2008), non-categorical similarity judgements were not found to be more accurate than identification decisions. In fact, at best, the accuracy of max similarity judgements was comparable to identification decisions (see Zwartz, 2016). However, despite these modest results, some evidence was found to suggest that similarity judgements might provide important and diagnostically relevant information to eyewitness researchers and triers of fact. For example, in lineups where there was high discrepancy (i.e., one lineup member stood out), the lineup member adjudged to be the most similar (similarity condition) was almost always (91%) identified (identification condition), and in most cases (94%), this lineup member was the target (Zwartz et al., 2024). These high levels of correspondence provide some tentative support for Zwartz's (2016) prior assertion that similarity serves as the "basis upon which more complex judgements regarding identity are made" (p. 117).

Although the initial findings provide some evidence to suggest that subjective perceptions of ecphoric similarity underpin categorical recognition decisions, it is important to recognise some of the limitations of the current knowledge base. Indeed, as there is only a single published paper exploring similarity judgements as an alternative to identification (Zwartz et al., 2024), there are many unresolved questions regarding the theoretical and practical utility of the similarity approach to lineup-based recognition. For example, regarding the theoretical utility of similarity judgements, it is difficult to assess claims that similarity judgements serve as a "relatively direct proxy" for confidence judgements (e.g., Sauer et al., 2012a), or "precede and inform" identification decisions and confidence judgements (Fitousi, 2024; Zwartz, 2016). Currently, there does not appear to be any published literature that has examined correspondence between the three recognition approaches in the context of the same lineup-based recognition task. In addition, because Zwartz et al. (2024) focused almost exclusively on comparing rates that targets were identified or received a unique max similarity judgement (i.e., the judgement with the highest numeric value in a lineup), there has been limited consideration for how patterns of max similarity judgements might reflect, or differ from, other identification decisions (e.g., foil and non-identifications). Expanding the scope of comparisons is theoretically important, as patterns of "accurate" similarity judgements obtained from target-present lineups may be reliant on, or driven by entirely different internal cognitive processes, than patterns of "accurate" similarity judgements from target-absent lineups (Fitousi, 2024; Fysh & Bindemann, 2023; Pozzulo & Lindsay, 1998). Notably, accuracy in target-present lineups could be driven by similarity processes (i.e., adjudging the target is highly similar), whereas accuracy in target-absent lineups could be driven by dissimilarity processes (i.e., adjudging that no lineup member is highly similar; Fitousi, 2024; Fysh & Bindemann, 2023; Johns & Mewhort, 2002; Mewhort & Johns, 2000; Stevens & Brown, 2005).

Regarding the practical utility of the similarity judgement approach, it remains unclear whether an approach like similarity that does not operate within a framework of identity (see Jordan, 2021) would ever be considered "reasonable or practicable" by eyewitness researchers or policymakers (Leippe & Wells, 1995). Detractors can and already have suggested that alternative approaches like similarity judgements are likely to be beset by numerous practical and legal challenges (see ALRC, 2006; Leippe & Wells, 1995). While such challenges should not be readily dismissed, we reason that an important first step on the path to acceptance could be to determine if similarity judgements enhance the capacity of witnesses to accurately discriminate correct from incorrect responses in lineup-based recognition tasks. As mentioned earlier in this chapter, eyewitness researchers have increasingly claimed that only discrimination measures should be used to inform "decisions made by policymakers about system variables that influence eyewitness decision making" (Mickes, 2015, p. 93). Although we do not entirely accept this position, prior research has not applied discrimination measures to similarity judgements (Jordan, 2021; Zwartz et al., 2024). As such, it is not currently known if similarity judgements can be used to accurately discriminate between correct and incorrect responses, or indeed, if similarity judgements can enhance discrimination relative to traditional, and other alternative (i.e., confidence judgements) approaches to lineup-based recognition.

Summary

In this chapter, we reviewed relevant psychological and legal literature that built directly on the key information presented in Chapter 1. We critically appraised the traditional identification approach while elaborating on the psychological and legal issues of identification. We also examined the roles of confidence and similarity judgements in recognition contexts and discussed the advent of both non-categorical approaches to obtaining eyewitness evidence from lineups. In Chapter 3, we highlight the importance of appearance in recognition contexts and outline our methodological approach to the research presented in this book.

References

Albright, T. D. (2016). Why eyewitnesses fail. *Proceedings of the National Academy of Sciences of the United States of America*, *114*(30), 7758–7764. https://doi.org/10.1073/pnas.1706891114

Australian Law Reform Commission. (1985). *Evidence: Volume 1. ALRC 26*. Retrieved from https://www.alrc.gov.au/publication/uniform-evidence-law-alrc-report-102/13-identification-evidence/background-identification-evidence-under-the-uniform-evidence-acts/

Australian Law Reform Commission. (2006). *Identification evidence*. Retrieved from www.alrc.gov.au/publications

Ayala, N. T., Smith, A. M., & Ying, R. C. (2022). The rule-out procedure: Increasing the potential for police investigators to detect suspect innocence from eyewitness lineup procedures. *Journal of Applied Research in Memory and Cognition*, *11*(4), 489–499. https://doi.org/10.1037/mac0000018

Baranski, J. V., & Petrusic, W. M. (2001). Testing architectures of the decision-confidence relation. *Canadian Journal of Experimental Psychology/Revue Canadienne de Psychologie Expérimentale*, *55*(3), 195–206. https://doi.org/10.1037/h0087366

Borthwell, R. K., Deffenbacher, K. A., & Brigham, J. C. (1987). Correlation of eyewitness accuracy and confidence: Optimality hypothesis revisited. *Journal of Applied Psychology*, *72*(3), 691–695. https://doi.org/10.1037/0021-9010.72.4.691

Brewer, N. (2006). Uses and abuses of eyewitness identification confidence. *Legal and Criminological Psychology*, *11*, 3–23. https://doi.org/10.1348/135532505X79672

Brewer, N., & Doyle, J. (2021). Changing the face of police lineups: Delivering more information from witnesses. *Journal of Applied Research in Memory and Cognition*, *10*(2), 180–195. https://doi.org/10.1016/j.jarmac.2020.12.004

Brewer, N., Weber, N., & Guerin, N. (2020). Police lineups of the future? *American Psychologist*, *75*(1), 76–91. https://doi.org/10.1037/amp0000465

Brewer, N., Weber, N., Wooton, D., & Lindsay, D. S. (2012). Identifying the bad guy in a lineup using confidence judgements under deadline pressure. *Psychological Science*, *23*(10), 1208–1214. https://doi.org/10.1177/0956797612441217

Brewer, N., & Wells, G. L. (2006). The confidence-accuracy relationship in eyewitness identification: Effects on lineup instructions, foil similarity, and target absent base rates. *Journal of Experimental Psychology*, *12*(1), 11–30. https://doi.org/10.1037/1076-898X.12.1.11

Brewer, N., & Wells, G. L. (2011). Eyewitness identification. *Current Directions in Psychological Science*, *20*(1), 24–27. https://doi.org/10.1177/0963721410389169

Bruer, K. C., Fitzgerald, R. J., Price, H. L., & Sauer, J. D. (2017). How sure are you that this is the man you saw? Child witnesses can use confidence judgments to identify a target. *Law and Human Behaviour*, *41*(6), 541–555. https://doi.org/10.1037/lhb0000260

Bruer, K. C., & Pozzulo, J. D. (2014). Influence of eyewitness age and recall error on mock juror decision-making. *Legal and Criminological Psychology*, *19*(2), 332–348. https://doi.org/10.1111/lcrp.12001

Carlson, C. A., Jones, A. R., Goodsell, C. A., Carlson, M. A., Weatherford, D. R., Whittington, J. E., & Lockamyier, R. F. (2019a). A method for increasing discriminability and eliminating top row preference in photo arrays. *Applied Cognitive Psychology*, *33*(6), 1091–1102. https://doi.org/10.1002/acp.3551

Carlson, C. A., Jones, A. R., Whittington, J. E., Lockamyeir, R. F., Carlson, M. A., & Wooten, A. R. (2019b). Lineup fairness: Propitious heterogeneity and the diagnostic feature detection hypothesis. *Cognitive Research: Principles and Implications*, *4*, 20. https://doi.org/10.1186/s41235-019-0185-0

Charman, S. D., & Wells, G. L. (2007). Eyewitness lineups: Is the appearance-change instruction a good idea? *Law and Human Behaviour*, *31*, 3–22. https://doi.org/10.1007/s10979-006-9006-3

Charman, S. D., & Wells, G. L. (2012). The moderating effects of ecphoric experience on post-identification feedback: A critical test of the cues-based inference conceptualisation. *Applied Cognitive Psychology*, *26*(2), 243–250. https://doi.org/10.1002/acp.1815

Charman, S. D., Shambaugh, L. J., Cahill, B. S., & Molinaro, P. F. (2022). The ability to infer witness accuracy from high-confidence lineup identifications is undermined by the appearance-change instruction and target appearance change. *Psychology, Public Policy, and Law*, *28*(4), 491–504. https://doi.org/10.1037/law0000368

Clark, S. E. (2011). Blackstone and the balance of eyewitness identification evidence. *Albany Law Review*, *74*(3), 1105. Retrieved from http://www.heinonline.org.ezproxy.ecu.edu.au/HOL/Page?public=false&handle=hein.journals/albany74&page=1105&collection=journals

Clark, S. E., Erickson, M. A., & Breneman, J. (2010). Probative value of absolute and relative judgements in eyewitness identification. *Law and Human Behaviour*, *35*(5), 364–380. https://doi.org/10.1007/s10979-010-9245-1

Clark, S. E., & Godfrey, R. (2009). Eyewitness identification evidence and innocence risk. *Psychonomic Bulletin & Review*, *16*, 22–42. https://doi.org/10.3758/pbr.16.1.22

Clark, S. E., & Gronlund, S. D. (1996). Global matching models of recognition memory. How the models match the data. *Psychonomic Bulletin & Review*, *3*(1), 37–60. https://doi.org/10.3758/BF03210740

Colloff, M. F., Wilson, B. M., & Flowe, H. D. (2021). Legal system v. Eyewitness: The jury is still out on who is better able to reduce eyewitness error (variance). *Journal of Applied Research in Memory and Cognition*, *10*(2), 200–204. https://doi.org/10.1016/j.jarmac.2021.04.001

Coyle, I. R., & Thomson, D. M. (2014). Opening up a can of worms: how do decision makers decide when witnesses are telling the truth? *Psychiatry, Psychology and Law*, *21*(4), 475–491. https://doi.org/10.1080/13218719.2013.837803

Cutler, B. L., & Penrod, S. D. (1988). Improving the reliability of eyewitness identification: Lineup construction ad presentation. *Journal of Applied Psychology*, *73*(2), 281–290. https://doi.org/10.1037/0021-9010.73.2.281

Cutler, B. L., Penrod, S. D., & Stuve, T. E. (1988). Juror decision making in eyewitness identification cases. *Law and Human Behaviour*, *12*(1), 41–55. https://doi.org/10.1007/bf01064273

Cutler, B. L., Penrod, S. D., & Martens, T. K. (1987). Improving the reliability of eyewitness identification: Putting context into context. *Journal of Applied Psychology*, *72*, 629–637. https://doi.org/10.1037/0021-9010.72.4.629

Davis, D., & Loftus, E. F. (2012). Inconsistencies between law and the limits of human cognition: The case of eyewitness identification. In L. Nadel & W. P. Sinnott-Armstrong (Eds.), *Memory and law* (pp. 29–58). Oxford University Press. https://doi.org/10.1093/acprof:oso/9780199920754.003.0002

Deffenbacher, K. A., & Loftus, E. F. (1982). Do jurors share a common understanding concerning eyewitness behaviour? *Law and Human Behaviour*, *6*(1), 15–30. https://doi.org/10.1007/bf01049310

Dobolyi, D. G., & Dodson, C. S. (2013). Eyewitness confidence in simultaneous and sequential lineups: A criterion shift account for mistaken identification overconfidence. *Journal of Experimental Psychology*, *19*(4), 345–357. https://doi.org/10.1037/a0034596

Dodson, C. S., & Garrett, B. L. (2021). Can we get over IDs? *Journal of Applied Research in Memory and Cognition*, *10*(2), 212–214. https://doi.org/10.1016/j.jarmac.2021.03.008

Dunn, J. (2004). Remember-know. *A matter of confidence. Psychological Review*, *111*(2), 524–542. https://doi.org/10.1037/0033-295X.111.2.524

Fisher, R. P. (2021). On the real-world benefits and costs of assessing confidence of suspects and fillers in lineups: Commentary on Brewer and Doyle (2021). *Journal of Applied Research in Memory and Cognition*, *10*(2), 205–207. https://doi.org/10.1016/j.jarmac.2021.04.002

Fitousi, D. (2024). A signal detection-based confidence-similarity model of face matching. *Psychological Review*, *131*(3), 625–663. https://doi.org/10.1037/rev0000435

Fitzgerald, R. J., Oriet, C., & Price, H. L. (2015). Suspect filler similarity in eyewitness lineups: A literature review and a novel methodology. *Law and Human Behaviour*, *39*(1), 62–74. https://doi.org/10.1037/lhb0000095

Fitzgerald, R. J., Price, H. L., Oriet, C., & Charman, S. D. (2013). The effect of suspect-filler similarity on eyewitness identification decisions: A meta-analysis. *Psychology, Public Policy, and Law*, *19*, 151–164. https://doi.org/10.1037/a0030618

Fysh, M. C., & Bindemann, M. (2023). Understanding face matching. *Quarterly Journal of Experimental Psychology*, *76*(4), 862–880. https://doi.org/10.1177/17470218221104476

Gepshtein, S., Wang, Y., He, F., Diep, D., & Albright, T. D. (2020). A perceptual scaling approach to eyewitness identification. *Nature Communications*, *11*(1), 1–10. https://doi.org/10.1038/s41467-020-17194-5

Giacona, A. M., Lampinen, J. M., & Anastasi, J. S. (2021). Estimator variables can matter even for high-confidence lineup identifications made under pristine conditions. *Law and Human Behavior*, *45*, 256–270. https://doi.org/10.1037/lhb0000381

Grabman, J. H., Dobolyi, D. G., Berelovich, N. L., & Dodson, C. S. (2019). Predicting high confidence errors in eyewitness memory: The role of face recognition ability, decision time and justifications. *Journal of Applied Research in Memory and Cognition*, *8*(2), 223–243. https://doi.org/10.1016/j.jarmac.2019.02.002

Halvorsen, V. (2004). Is it better that ten guilty persons go free than that one innocent person be convicted? *Criminal Justice Ethics*, *23*(2), 3–13. http://doi.org/10.1080/0731129X.2004.9992168

Heller, J. (2006). The cognitive psychology of circumstantial evidence. *Michigan Law Review*, *105*(2), 24. Retrieved from http://www.jstor.org.ezproxy.ecu.edu.au/stable/40041577

Hiatt, L., & Trafton, J. (2017). Familiarity, priming, and perception in similarity judgements. *Cognitive Science*, *41*(6), 1450–1484. https://doi.org/10.1111/cogs.12418

Horry, R., & Brewer, N. (2016). How target-lure similarity shapes confidence judgments in multiple-alternative decision tasks. *Journal of Experimental Psychology: General, 145*(12), 1615–1634. https://doi.org/10.1037/xge0000227

Houston, K., Hope, L., Memon, A., & Read, D. (2013). Expert testimony on eyewitness evidence: In search of common sense. *Behavioural Sciences and the Law, 31*, 637–651. https://doi.org/10.1002/bsl.2080

Huang, C., & Fitzgerald, R. J. (2023, March 16–18). *An alternative approach to the rule-out lineup procedure* [Conference Session]. *American Psychology-Law Society Annual Conference*, Philadelphia, PA, United States. https://ap-ls.org/conferences/schedule.html

Innocence Project. (2013). *Innocence network exoneration report*. Retrieved from https://innocencenetwork.org/resources/innocence-collateral/network-exoneration-reports/innocence-network-exoneration-report-2013/view

Innocence Project. (2016). *The cases*. Retrieved from http://www.innocenceproject.org/all-cases/#eyewitness-misidentification, exonerated-by-dna.

Innocence Project. (2020). *Explore the numbers: Innocence Project's impact*. Retrieved from https://innocenceproject.org/exonerations-data/

Johns, E., & Mewhort, D. (2002). What information underlies correct rejections in short-term recognition memory? *Memory and Cognition, 30*, 46–59. Retrieved from https://doi.org/10.3758/BF03195264

Jordan, D. T. (2021). *Identity: A crisis of confidence? Or is it resemblance? An exploration of the different approaches by which eyewitness evidence can be obtained from lineups*. [Doctoral thesis, Edith Cowan University]. Research Online Institutional Repository https://ro.ecu.edu.au/theses/2449

Jordan, D. T., Scott, A. J., & Thomson, D. M. (2025). Appearances can be deceiving: How naturalistic changes to target appearance impact on lineup-based decision making. *Psychology, Crime & Law, 31*(4), 1–28. https://doi.org/10.1080/1068316X.2023.2243001

Juslin, P., Olsson, N., & Winman, A. (1996). Calibration and diagnosticity of confidence in eyewitness identification: Comments on what can be inferred from the low confidence accuracy correlation. *Journal of Experimental Psychology, 22*(5), 1304–1316. https://doi.org/10.1037/0278-7393.22.5.1304

Kantner, J., Dobbins, I. (2019). Partitioning the sources of recognition confidence: The role of individual differences. *Psychonomic Bulletin & Review, 26*, 1317–1324. https://doi.org/10.3758/s13423-019-01586-w

Kantner, J., & Lindsay, D. S. (2012). Response bias in recognition memory as a cognitive trait. *Memory & Cognition, 40*(8), 1163–1177. https://doi.org/10.3758/s13421-012-0226-0

Kaplan, A., & Medin, D. (1997). The coincidence effect in similarity and choice. *Memory and Cognition, 25*(4), 570–576. https://doi.org/10.3758/BF03201130

Koriat, A., & Goldsmith, M. (1996). Monitoring and control processes in the strategic regulation of memory accuracy. *Psychological Review, 103*(3), 490–517. https://doi.org/10.1037/0033-295x.103.3.490

Lampinen, J. M., Smith, A. M., & Wells, G. L. (2018). Four utilities in eyewitness identification practice: Dissociations between receiver operating characteristic analysis and expected utility analysis. *Law and Human Behavior*, *43*(1), 26–44. https://doi.org/10.1037/lhb0000309

Lampinen, J. M., Erickson, W. B., Moore, K. N., & Hittson, A. (2014). Effects of distance on face recognition: Implications for eyewitness identification. *Psychonomic Bulletin & Review*, *21*(6), 1489–1494. https://doi.org/10.3758/s13423-014-0641-2

Larkey, L., & Markman, A. (2005). Processes of similarity judgement. *Cognitive Science*, *29*(6), 1061–1076. https://doi.org/10.1207/s15516709cog0000_30

Leippe, M. R. (1995). The case for expert testimony about eyewitness memory. *Psychology, Public Policy and Law*, *1*(4), 909–959. https://doi.org/10.1037/1076-8971.1.4.909

Leippe, M. R., Eisenstadt, D., & Rauch, S. M. (2009). Cueing confidence in eyewitness identifications: Influence of biased lineup instructions and pre-identification memory feedback under varying lineup conditions. *Law and Human Behaviour*, *33*, 194–212. https://doi.org/10.1007/s10979-008-9135-y

Leippe, M. R., & Wells, G. L. (1995). Should we be partial to partial identification? A commentary on the Levi-Jungman proposal. *Criminal Justice and Behaviour*, *22*(4), 373–385. https://doi.org/10.1177/0093854895022004002

Levi, A. M. (2006). An analysis of multiple choices in MSL lineups, and a comparison with simultaneous and sequential ones. *Psychology, Crime & Law*, *12*(3), 273–285. https://doi.org/10.1080/10683160500238782

Levi, A. M., & Jungman, N. (1995). The police lineup: Basic weaknesses and radical solutions. *Criminal Justice and Behaviour*, *22*(4), 347–372. https://doi.org/10.1177/0093854895022004001

Lindsay, R. C., Semmler, C., Weber, N., Brewer, N., & Lindsay, M. R. (2008). How variations in distance affect eyewitness reports and identification accuracy. *Law and Human Behavior*, *32*(6), 526–535. https://doi.org/10.1007/s10979-008-9128-x

Malmberg, K. (2008). Recognition memory: A review of the critical findings and an integrated theory for relating them. *Cognitive Psychology*, *57*, 335–384. https://doi.org/10.1016/j.cogpsych.2008.02.004

Malpass, R. S., & Lindsay, R. C. L. (1999). Measuring line-up fairness. *Applied Cognitive Psychology*, *13*(Spec Issue), S1–S7. https://doi.org/10.1002/(SICI)1099-0720(199911)13:1+<S1::AID-ACP678>3.0.CO;2-9

Malpass, R. S., Tredoux, C. G., & McQuiston-Surrett, D. E. (2007). Lineup construction and lineup fairness. In R. C. L. Lindsay, D. F. Ross, J. D. Read & M. P. Toglia (Eds.), *The handbook of eyewitness psychology (Vol. II): Memory for people*. Lawrence Erlbaum & Associates.

Markman, A., & Medin, D. (1995). Similarity and alignment in choice. *Organisational Behaviour and Human Decision Processes*, *63*(2), 117–130. https://doi.org/10.1006/obhd.1995.1067

Martschuk, N., Sporer, S. L., & Sauerland, M. (2019). Confidence of older eyewitnesses: Is it diagnostic of identification accuracy? *Open Psychology*, *1*, 132–151. https://doi.org/10.1515/psych-2018-0010

McGuire, M., Kenny, T., & Grabic, A. (2015). Eyewitness identification for prudent policing. *An International Journal of Police Strategies and Management*, *38*(4), 598–609. https://doi.org/10.1108/PIJPSM-05-2015-0055

Medin, D., Goldstone, R., & Gentner, D. (1990). Similarity involving attributes and relations: Judgments of similarity and difference are not inverses. *Psychological Science*, *1*(1), 64–69. https://doi.org/10.1111/j.1467-9280.1990.tb00069.x

Medin, D., Goldstone, R., & Gentner, D. (1993). Respects for similarity. *Psychological Review*, *100*(2), 254–278. https://doi.org/10.1037/0033-295X.100.2.254

Medin, D., Goldstone, R., & Markman, A. (1995). Comparison and choice: Relations between similarity processes and decision processes. *Psychonomic Bulletin & Review*, *2*(1), 1–19. https://doi.org/10.3758/BF03214410

Mewhort, D., & Johns, E. (2000). The extralist-feature effect: Evidence against item matching in short-term recognition memory. *Journal of Experimental Psychology General*, *129*(2), 262–284. https://doi.org/10.1037/0096-3445.129.2.262

Mickes, L. (2015). Receiver operating characteristic analysis and confidence-accuracy characteristic analysis in investigations of system variables and estimator variables that effect eyewitness memory. *Journal of Applied Research in Memory and Cognition*, *4*, 93–105. https://doi.org/10.1016/j.jarmac.2015.01.003

Mickes, L., Flowe, H. D., & Wixted, J. T. (2012). Receiver operating characteristic analysis of eyewitness memory: Comparing the diagnostic accuracy of simultaneous versus sequential lineups. *Journal of Experimental Psychology*, *18*(4), 361–376. https://doi.org/10.1037/a0030609

Mu, E., Chung, T., & Reed, L. (2017). Paradigm shift in criminal police lineups: Eyewitness identification as multi-criteria decision making. *International Journal of Production Economics*, *184*, 95–106. https://doi.org/10.1016/j.ijpe.2016.11.019

Navon, D. (1990). How critical is the accuracy of an eyewitness's memory? Another look at the issue of lineup diagnosticity. *Journal of Applied Psychology*, *75*(5), 506–510. https://doi.org/10.1037/0021-9010.75.5.506

Newirth, K. A. (2021). The change to make change: A call for a moratorium on the admissibility of eyewitness identification evidence. *Journal of Applied Research in Memory and Cognition*, *10*(2), 225–228. https://doi.org/10.1016/j.jarmac.2021.05.004

Osgood, C. (1949). The similarity paradox in human learning: A resolution. *Psychological Review*, *56*(3), 132–143. https://doi.org/10.1037/h0057488

Oxford Shorter Dictionary. (2007). *Shorter Oxford English dictionary* (6th ed.). Oxford University Press.

Palmer, M. A., Brewer, N., Weber, N., & Nagesh, A. (2013). The confidence accuracy relationship for eyewitness identification decisions: Effects of exposure duration, retention interval and divided attention. *Journal of Experimental Psychology*, *19*(1), 55–71. https://doi.org/10.1037/a0031602

Paterson, H., Anderson, D., & Kemp, R. (2013). Cautioning jurors regarding co-witness discussion: The impact of judicial warnings. *Psychology, Crime and Law*, *19*(3), 287–304. https://doi.org/10.1080/1068316X.2011.631539

Petrusic, W. M., & Baranski, J. V. (2003). Judging confidence influences decision processing in comparative judgments. *Psychonomic Bulletin & Review*, *10*(1), 177–183. https://doi.org/10.3758/BF03196482

Pozzulo, J. D., & Dempsey, J. L. (2009). Witness factors and their influence on juror's perceptions and verdicts. *Criminal Justice and Behaviour*, *36*(9), 923–934. https://doi.org/10.1177/0093854809338450

Pozzulo, J. D., Lemieux, J. M., Wells, E., & McCuaig, H. J. (2006). The influence of eyewitness identification decisions and age of witness on juror's verdicts and perceptions of reliability. *Psychology, Crime and Law*, *12*(6), 641–652. https://doi.org/10.1080/10683160500415539

Pozzulo, J. D., & Lindsay, R. C. L. (1998). Identification accuracy of children versus adults: A meta-analysis. *Law and Human Behavior*, *22*(5), 549–570. https://doi.org/10.1023/A:1025739514042

Price, H. L., & Fitzgerald, R. J. (2015). Face-off: A new identification procedure for child eyewitnesses. *Journal of Experimental Psychology: Applied*, *22*(3), 366–380. https://doi.org/10.1037/xap0000091

Reardon, M. C., & Fisher, R. P. (2011). Effect of viewing the interview and identification process on juror perceptions of eyewitness accuracy. *Applied Cognitive Psychology*, *25*(1), 68–77. https://doi.org/10.1002/acp.1643

Ross, S. (2008). *Processing facial similarity: Utilizing denotative and connotative information to understand facial similarity judgments*. Retrieved from https://scholarworks.utep.edu/dissertations/AAI3310674/

Rossmo, D. K. (2021). Delivering more information to and from lineup witnesses: Commentary on Brewer and Doyle. *Journal of Applied Research in Memory and Cognition*, *10*(2), 196–199. https://doi.org/10.1016/j.jarmac.2021.03.004

Sauer, J. D., & Brewer, N. (2015). Confidence and accuracy of eyewitness identification. In T. Valentine, & J. Davis *Forensic facial identification: Theory and practice of identification from eyewitnesses, composites and CCTV* (pp. 185–208). Wiley Blackwell.

Sauer, J. D., Brewer, N., & Weber, N. (2008). Multiple confidence estimates as indices of eyewitness memory. *Journal of Experimental Psychology*, *137*(3), 528–547. https://doi.org/10.1037/a0012712

Sauer, J. D., Brewer, N., & Weber, N. (2012b). Using confidence ratings to identify a target among foils. *Journal of Applied Research in Memory and Cognition*, *1*, 80–88. https://doi.org/10.1016/j.jarmac.2012.03.003

Sauer, J. D., Brewer, N., Zweck, T., & Weber, N. (2010). The effect of retention interval on the confidence and accuracy relationship for eyewitness identification. *Law and Human Behaviour*, *34*, 337–347. https://doi.org/10.1007/s10979-009-9192-x

Sauer, J. D., Palmer, M., & Brewer, N. (2019). Eyewitness identification. In N. Brewer & A. Douglas (Eds.), *Psychological science and the law*. Guilford Press.

Sauer, J. D., Weber, N., & Brewer, N. (2012a). Using ecphoric confidence ratings to discriminate seen from unseen faces: The effects of retention interval and distinctiveness. *Psychonomic Bulletin and Review*, *19*, 490–498. https://doi.org/10.3758/s13423-012-0239-5

Sauerland, M., Sagana, A., & Sporer, S. L. (2012). Assessing non-choosers eyewitness identification accuracy from photographic showups by using confidence and response time. *Law and Human Behaviour*, *36*(5), 394–403. https://doi.org/10.1037/h0093926

Seale-Carlisle, T. M. (2024). Improving the diagnostic value of lineup rejections. *Cognition* [Advance Online Publication]. https://doi.org/10.1016/j.cognition.2024.105917

Seelau, E. (1995). *Ecphoric similarity and confidence judgements of eyewitnesses: Effects of extra-memorial information*. [Doctoral thesis Iowa State University]. Iowa State University Digital Repository. https://dr.lib.iastate.edu/handle/20.500.12876/64188/

Selmeczy, D., & Dobbins, I. G. (2013). Metacognitive awareness and adaptive recognition biases. *Journal of Experimental Psychology: Learning, Memory, and Cognition*, *39*(3), 678–690. https://doi.org/10.1037/a0029469

Semmler, C., Brewer, N., & Douglass, A. B. (2011). Jurors believe eyewitnesses. In B. L. Cutler (Ed.), *Conviction of the innocent: Lessons from psychological research* (p. 185–209). American Psychological Association. https://doi.org/10.1037/13085-009

Semmler, C., Dunn, J., Mickes, L., & Wixted, J. T. (2018). The role of estimator variables in eyewitness identification. *Journal of Experimental Psychology: Applied*, *24*(3), 400. https://doi.org/10.1037/xap0000157

Shen, K. J., Huang, J., Lam, A. L., & Wixted, J. T. (2024). The effects of filler similarity and lineup size on eyewitness identification. *Journal of experimental psychology. Learning, memory, and cognition*, *50*(9), 1444–1462. https://doi.org/10.1037/xlm0001342

Smith, A. M., & Leach, A. (2019). Confidence can be used to discriminate between accurate and inaccurate lie decisions. *Perspectives on Psychological Science*, *14*(6), 1062–1071. https://doi.org/10.1177/1745691619863431

Smith, A. M., Wilford, M. M., Quigley-McBride, A., & Wells, G. L. (2019). Mistaken eyewitness identification rates increase when either witnessing or testing conditions get worse. *Law and Human Behaviour*, *43*(4), 358–368. https://doi.org/10.1037/lhb0000334

Smith, A. M., & Ayala, N. T. (2021). Do traditional lineups undermine the capacity for eyewitness memory to rule out innocent suspects? *Journal of Applied Research in Memory and Cognition*, *10*(2), 215–220. https://doi.org/10.1016/j.jarmac.2021.03.003

Smith, A. M., Ayala, N. T., & Ying, R. C. (2023). The rule out procedure: A signal-detection-informed approach to the collection of eyewitness identification evidence. *Psychology, Public Policy, and Law*, *29*(1), 19–31. https://doi.org/10.1037/law0000373

Sporer, S. L., Penrod, S. D., Read, D., & Cutler, B. L. (1995). Choosing, confidence and accuracy: A meta-analysis of the confidence-accuracy relation in eyewitness identification studies. *Psychological Bulletin*, *118*(3), 315–327. https://doi.org/10.1037/0033-2909.118.3.315

Steblay, N. K., & Brooks, W. G. III. (2021). Practical concerns for investigations and courtroom: A commentary on Brewer and Doyle (2021). *Journal of Applied Research in Memory and Cognition*, *10*(2), 208–211. https://doi.org/10.1016/j.jarmac.2021.03.005

Steblay, N. K., & Wells, G. L. (2020). Assessment of bias in police lineups. *Psychology, Public Policy, and Law*, *26*(4), 393–412. https://doi.org/10.1037/law0000287

Stevens, N., & Brown, D. (2005). Similarity and dissimilarity as evidence in perceptual categorization. *Journal of Mathematical Psychology*, *49*(5), 403–409. https://doi.org/10.1016/j.jmp.2005.06.001

Thomson, D. M. (1982). The realities of eyewitness identification. *Australian Journal of Forensic Sciences*, *14*, 150–157. https://doi.org/10.1080/00450618209411171

Thomson, D. M. (1986). Face recognition: More than a feeling of familiarity? In H. D. Ellis, M. A. Jeeves, F. Newcombe & A. Young (Eds.), *Aspects of Face Processing* (pp. 391–399). Elsevier.

Thomson, D. M. (1989). *Psychological fiction in the court room: And they did not live happily ever after. Unpublished Manuscript*. Monash University: Melbourne.

Tredoux, C. G. (2002). A direct measure of facial similarity and its relation to human similarity perceptions. *Journal of Experimental Psychology: Applied*, *8*(3), 180–193. https://doi.org/10.1037//1076-898x.8.3.180

Tulving, E. (1981). Similarity relations in recognition. *Journal of Verbal Learning and Verbal Behaviour*, *20*, 479–496. https://doi.org/10.1016/S0022-5371(81)90129-8

Tulving, E. (1983). Ecphoric processes in episodic memory. *Philosophical Transactions of the Royal Society of Biological Sciences*, *302*(1110), 361–371. https://doi.org/10.1098/rstb.1983.0060

Tversky, A. (1977). Features of similarity. *Psychological Review*, *84*(4), 327–352. https://doi.org/10.1037/0033-295X.84.4.327

Tversky, A., & Gati, I. (1982). Similarity, separability, and the triangle inequality. *Psychological Review*, *89*(2), 123–154. https://doi.org/10.1037/0033-295X.89.2.123

Van Zandt, T. (2000). ROC curves and confidence judgments in recognition memory. *Journal of Experimental Psychology: Learning, Memory, and Cognition*, *26*, 582–600. https://doi.org/10.1037//0278-7393.26.3.582

Vickers, D. (1979). *Decision processes in visual perception*. Academic Press.

Weber, N., & Varga, M. (2012). Can a modified lineup improve the usefulness of confidence? *Journal of Applied Research in Memory and Cognition*, *1*, 152–157. https://doi.org/10.1016/j.jarmac.2012.06.007

Merriam Webster. (2025). *Merriam Webster Dictionary*. Retrieved https://www.merriam-webster.com/

Wells, G. L. (1993). What do we know about eyewitness identification? *American Psychologist*, *48*(5), 553–571. https://doi.org/10.1037/0003-066X.48.5.553

Wells, G. L. (2014). Eyewitness identification: Probative value, criterion shifts and policy regarding the sequential lineup. *Current Directions in Psychological Science*, *23*(1), 11–16. https://doi.org/10.1177/0963721413504781

Wells, G. L., Kovera, M. B., Douglass, A. B., Brewer, N., Meissner, C. A., & Wixted, J. T. (2020). Policy and procedure recommendations for the collection and preservation of eyewitness identification evidence. *Law and Human Behaviour*, *44*(1), 3–36. https://doi.org/10.1037/lhb0000359

Wells, G. L., Memon, A., & Penrod, S. D. (2006). Eyewitness evidence: Improving its probative value. *Psychological Science in the Public Interest*, *30*, 45–75. https://doi.org/10.1111/j.1529-1006.2006.00027.x

Wells, G. L., & Olson, E. A. (2003). Eyewitness testimony. *Annual Review of Psychology*, *54*(1), 277–285. https://doi.org/10.1146/annurev.psych.54.101601.145028

Wells, G. L., & Quinlivan, D. S. (2009). Suggestive eyewitness identification procedures and the Supreme Court's reliability test in light of eyewitness science: 30 years later. *Law and Human Behavior*, *33*(1), 1–24. https://doi.org/10.1007/s10979-008-9130-3

Wixted, J. T. (2007). Dual process theory and signal detection theory of recognition memory. *Psychological Review*, *114*(1), 152–176. https://doi.org/10.1037/0033-295X.114.1.152

Wixted, J. T., Mickes, L., Clark, S. E., Gronlund, S. D., & Roedigar, H. L. (2015). Initial eyewitness confidence reliably predicts eyewitness identification accuracy. *American Psychologist*, *70*(6), 515–526. https://doi.org/10.1037/a0039510

Wixted, J. T., Mickes, L., Dunn, J. C., & Wells, W. (2016). Estimating the reliability of eyewitness identifications from police lineups. *Psychological and Cognitive Sciences*, *113*(2), 304–309. https://doi.org/10.1073/pnas.1516814112

Wixted, J. T., & Wells, G. L. (2017). The relationship between eyewitness confidence and identification accuracy: A new synthesis. *Psychological Science in the Public Interest*, *18*, 10–65. https://doi.org/10.1177/1529100616686966

Yeung, N., & Summerfield, C. (2012). Metacognition in human decision making: Confidence and error monitoring. *Philosophical Transactions of the Society of Biological Sciences*, *367*(1594), 1310–1321. https://doi.org/10.1098/rstb.2011.0416

Yilmaz, A. S., Wilson, B. M., & Wixted, J. T. (2025). A Rate-them-all lineup procedure increases information and reduces discriminability. *Journal of Experimental Psychology: Applied*, *31*(1), 1–11. https://doi.org/10.1037/xap0000524

Zwartz, M. (2016). *Identity crisis in identification evidence: Similarity judgements as an alternative to identification decisions*. [Doctoral thesis, Deakin University]. Research Online Institutional Repository. http://dro.deakin.edu.au

Zwartz, M., Thomson, D. M., & Scott, A. J. (2024). Identity crisis in eyewitness testimony: Exploring visual similarity judgments as an alternative to identification decisions. *Criminal Law Journal*, *47*(2), 93–108.

3 Appearance and Methodology

In this chapter, we discuss the role of appearance in recognition contexts and outline our methodological approach to the research presented in this book. This chapter is divided into two related but distinct sections. In the first section, we highlight the role of appearance in recognition contexts and provide a critical review of literature examining the influence of target appearance change(s) on identification decisions. We also explain the relevance of appearance when examining the theoretical and practical utility of the traditional identification approach, and two alternative approaches to obtaining eyewitness evidence from lineups: Non-categorical confidence judgements and non-categorical similarity judgements. In the second section, we provide information regarding the participants, design, materials, and procedure of our research. Additional information regarding our analytical approach is provided in Chapters 4 and 5.

Appearance in Recognition Contexts

In recognition contexts, appearance describes the relationship between contextual cues stored at encoding and contextual cues available at retrieval. In this book, we examine two states of target appearance: No-change, where contextual cues relating to appearance are maintained between encoding and retrieval; and change, where contextual cues relating to appearance are altered in the interval between encoding and retrieval. Previously, the third author distinguished between general contextual factors (i.e., background and action) and person-specific contextual factors (i.e., clothing and appearance), in their research examining the effects of context on person identification (e.g., Thomson et al., 1982). The appearance change manipulation described in this book involved the alteration of three person-specific contextual factors: Cranial hair, facial hair, and clothing.

In lineup-based recognition contexts, changes to person-specific contextual factors have typically been classified as either disguise-related or

DOI: 10.4324/9781003569923-3

naturalistic (Hope & Sauer, 2014; Jordan et al., 2025). Disguise-related changes involve the deliberate addition or removal of paraphernalia worn to obscure salient parts of a perpetrator's underlying facial structure (Cutler et al., 1987; Mansour et al., 2020; O'Rourke et al., 1989). Naturalistic changes occur with the passage of time, and involve alterations to cranial hair length, colour and style, facial hair length or presence (in male populations), body shape, weight, and age (Charman & Wells, 2007). While our target appearance manipulation involved naturalistic changes, to date, most research has focused on disguise-related changes (see Lee, 2019). Therefore, we review literature examining the impact of both disguise-related and naturalistic changes to appearance on recognition.

The Effect of Appearance Change

In a criminal investigation, police officers rarely apprehend the perpetrator at the scene of a crime (Pozzulo & Balfour, 2006; Pozzulo & Marciniak, 2006), resulting in a delay between the witnessed criminal event and subsequent lineup-based identification. During this delay, the appearance of a perpetrator can change (Terry, 1994; Thomson, 1982). We believe that the appearance characteristics of a perpetrator play a critical role in recognition, for in the absence of familiarity or prior knowledge of a perpetrator's identity, person-specific contextual cues associated with their appearance are the main source of information available to witnesses when responding to a lineup-based recognition task (Jordan et al., 2025; Thomson, 1982, 1989).

Understandably, a considerable amount of literature has sought to examine the effect that altering or obscuring a person's appearance has on recognition accuracy (Baddeley & Woodhead, 1982; Bruce, 1982; Bruce et al., 1987; Diamond & Carey, 1977; Lander & Bruce, 2003; McKelvie, 1991; Seitz, 2003). In the broader recognition literature, appearance changes involving alterations in expression (Diamond & Carey, 1977), pose (Baddeley & Woodhead, 1982; Seitz, 2003), presentation (McKelvie, 1991), movement (Lander & Bruce, 2003), clothing (Thomson et al., 1982), and facial paraphernalia (Righi et al., 2012) have all been found to reduce a participant's capacity to correctly discriminate (i.e., accurately distinguish) a stimulus they have encountered before from one that they have not (i.e., a face seen previously or not; see Shapiro & Penrod, 1986).

Similar outcomes have been observed in lineup-based recognition contexts. For example, research has consistently found that disguise-related changes have a significant deleterious effect on identification accuracy in target-present lineups (Lee, 2019). In fact, the addition and removal of glasses (Mansour et al., 2020), hats (Cutler et al., 1987; O'Rourke et al., 1989) and other disguise-related changes, such as wigs (Pozzulo & Balfour, 2006; Pozzulo & Marciniak, 2006; Yarmey, 2004) and masks (Davies & Flin, 1984; Manley et al., 2021; Palu et al., 2023), have all been found to significantly reduce the proportion of correct target identifications. The limited research examining the impact of naturalistic changes has produced similar findings. Changes to cranial (Memon & Gabbert, 2003) and facial hair length or presence (Gronlund et al., 2009; Jordan et al., 2025), as well as those that occur naturally over a 12-month period (Charman et al., 2022; Molinaro et al., 2013), have all produced large declines in the proportion of correct target identifications. Interestingly, appearance changes have been found to have a similar detrimental impact on identification accuracy irrespective of whether they reflect "relatively subtle" day-to-day variations or the use of deliberate and distinct disguises (e.g., Gronlund et al., 2009; Jordan et al., 2024, 2025).

Theoretical accounts of recognition, such as signal detection theory, offer an explanation as to why correct target identifications diminish when targets change their appearance. As discussed in Chapter 2, signal detection accounts posit that the process of making an identification decision is dependent on the interaction between two internal cognitive processes: Match-to-memory and decision criterion (i.e., a pre-set internal threshold for responding; Baranski & Petrusic, 2001; Sauer et al., 2008). As we and other researchers have argued, in cases involving unknown perpetrators, appearance constitutes the main source of perceptual, and by extension, memorial, information available to witnesses when responding to a line-up-based recognition task (Charman & Wells, 2007; Jordan et al., 2025; Thomson, 1982). A changed perpetrator will, therefore, generate less match-to-memory information than an unchanged perpetrator when presented as part of a lineup, because fewer perceptual cues are available at retrieval to act as reliable markers of recognition (Shapiro & Penrod, 1986; Thomson, 1986; Thomson et al., 1982). In signal detection terms, changing perpetrator appearance directly weakens match-to-memory signal strength, making it less likely to exceed a witness's decision criterion and trigger a positive identification (Jordan et al., 2025).

Basic theories of face processing provide a similar explanation to signal detection accounts. According to face processing accounts, changing target appearance between encoding and retrieval can disrupt a participant's holistic processing system (Chung & Thomson, 1995; Maurer et al., 2002; Nakabayashi & Liu, 2014). Holistic processing occurs when individuals process the space and relationship between features on a face and encode it into memory as a gestalt or configurational whole (Chung & Thomson, 1995; Maurer et al., 2002). According to several researchers, altering a single feature (e.g., cranial hair) or texture (e.g., facial hair) on an unfamiliar face can influence its perceived configurational properties (Macrae & Lewis, 2002; Maurer et al., 2002; Navon, 1977; Perfect, 2003; Perfect et al., 2007). This has a detrimental impact on recognition, for if the visual configuration of the target available at retrieval does not adequately match the previously stored configuration of the target encoded in memory, then this pattern is unlikely to be recognised as the "same" and thus will likely fail to trigger a positive identification (Perfect et al., 2007).

While the effect of appearance in target-present lineups has been well-established, comparatively little attention has been afforded to appearance in target-absent lineups (Mansour et al., 2020). Perhaps this is because participants only view a single representation of the target at encoding, and therefore, no actual change is made to target appearance in target-absent lineups (Jordan et al., 2025). Instead, *change* typically describes a condition whereby members of the lineup do not resemble or match the general description of the target presented during encoding (Charman et al., 2022; Jordan et al., 2025; Pozzulo & Balfour, 2006). Specifically, lineup members are selected on the basis that they resemble or match a description of the target presented in the no-change condition. Thus, if the change involves the addition of facial hair at encoding, lineup members would be selected on the basis that they match or resemble the target without facial hair.

Pozzulo and colleagues suggested that witnesses should be able to reject target-absent lineups more easily in change conditions, as there are generally fewer similarities between lineup members, including target replacements (replacements), and targets that can resonate in memory (Pozzulo & Balfour, 2006; Pozzulo & Marciniak, 2006). While the authors' suggestion is logical, surprisingly, target appearance has rarely been found to increase correct non-identifications in target-absent conditions. In fact, appearance has either been found to have no effect on target-absent identification decisions (Jordan et al., 2025; Pozzulo & Balfour, 2006; Pozzulo & Marciniak, 2006; Yarmey, 2004), or less frequently, increase incorrect replacement and foil identifications (Mansour et al., 2020).

Increased incorrect replacement and foil identifications in change conditions have been tentatively attributed to a strength-based mirror effect (Mansour et al., 2020; Smith et al., 2019). According to this effect, varying the quality or quantity of visual cues (i.e., target appearance) between encoding and retrieval can encourage participants to reduce the degree of evidence required to trigger an identification (Criss, 2006; Stretch & Wixted, 1998). Specifically, in conditions where the memorial experience is particularly weak (i.e., target absent, change conditions), some participants may adjust their decision criterion to reflect the smaller amount of memorial evidence available. It is not clear why the effect of appearance on target-absent decisions varies between studies; however, variability in the methodological design (e.g., how appearance has been manipulated) has likely contributed to some of these discrepancies.

Theoretical and Practical Relevance of Appearance

Research has consistently shown that changed targets are recognised significantly less often than unchanged targets (e.g., Cutler et al., 1987;

Gronlund et al., 2009; Jordan et al., 2025; Lee, 2019; Memon & Gabbert, 2003; Pozzulo & Balfour, 2006; Pozzulo & Marciniak, 2006; O'Rourke et al., 1989; Shapiro & Penrod, 1986), providing compelling evidence to suggest that people cannot easily look beyond appearance to establish identity. Indeed, in empirical research, many participants appear to mistakenly adjudge that a changed target is a different person from the target seen at encoding, as opposed to the same person with different features (e.g., Jordan et al., 2025). The relatively uniform effect of appearance in target-present lineups has been labelled by some researchers as "fairly predictable" (e.g., Clark & Godfrey, 2009); ostensibly because appearance constitutes the main source of memorial information available to participants in responding to a lineup-based recognition task when the target is an unfamiliar person (Charman & Wells, 2007). It is for this reason that appearance is a logical factor for exploring the theoretical relationships that exist between identity, confidence, and similarity.

As discussed in Chapter 2, theoretical accounts of recognition, confidence, and similarity processing posit that all three recognition constructs access and rely on match-to-memory information (Baranski & Petrusic, 2001; Clark, 2011; Jordan, 2021; Sauer et al., 2008). According to these same accounts, manipulating or changing appearance in the interval between encoding and retrieval represents a direct manipulation of match-to-memory signal strength (see Charman & Wells, 2007, 2012). Therefore, if confidence and similarity judgements rely on the same match-to-memory information as identification, they should be similarly sensitive to manipulations of appearance. The small number of studies examining the impact of appearance on post-decisional confidence ratings (i.e., the certainty participants have in the accuracy of an identification decision) have found that confidence in correct identifications from target-present lineups often declines in change conditions (e.g., Gronlund et al., 2009; Jordan et al., 2025; Mansour et al., 2020). These findings suggest that post-decisional confidence ratings index memory strength information and are sensitive to changes in the memorial experience. Non-categorical confidence and similarity judgements have been presented as distinct, and potentially more direct measures of match-to-memory than post-decisional confidence ratings (Sauer et al., 2012; Zwartz, 2016). However, these claims have received limited attention with respect to appearance, or more specifically, appearance change (Jordan et al., 2025). To our knowledge, no published research has examined the influence of appearance on non-categorical approaches to lineup-based recognition. Therefore, to develop novel insights into the associations between the three recognition approaches, it is important to establish how appearance interacts, or affects, measures of evidence strength information, specifically confidence and similarity judgements.

Appearance as a manipulation is theoretically important, but the practical influence of appearance change should not be overlooked. As several researchers have acknowledged, appearance changes often occur on a day-to-day basis and, therefore, could play a role in many criminal investigations and lineup-based recognition tasks (Charman et al., 2022; Erickson et al., 2017; Jordan et al., 2025). Further, there is no way to account for the occurrence of appearance change in real-world contexts because recognising that a perpetrator has undergone a change (or changes) is often conditional on first recognising that the suspect is the perpetrator (Charman et al., 2022). Given that relatively subtle, naturalistic changes have a sizeable impact on identifications and post-decisional confidence (Gronlund et al., 2009; Jordan et al., 2024), we believe it is important that researchers explore if alternative approaches are as susceptible to the influence of appearance as traditional categorical identification decisions (see Jordan et al., 2025).

It is worth reiterating here that the theoretical assumptions presented throughout this book suggest responses collected using traditional and alternative approaches (i.e., identification decisions, confidence judgements, and similarity judgements) to obtaining eyewitness evidence from lineups should all be sensitive to the influence of appearance. However, for practical purposes, it is important to examine if alternative approaches offer any improvements in response accuracy or, more importantly, provide richer and more diagnostic sources of evidence in conditions where target appearance changes (i.e., when memorial information is weaker).

Methodological Approach

In this section, we provide information regarding the participants, design, materials, and procedure of our research. Importantly, the research presented in this book utilises data collected as part of the first author's PhD (Jordan, 2021). However, this book extends on the original work by providing a novel and refined exploration of the variables with the greatest theoretical and applied implications (i.e., recognition approach, target appearance, and target presence).

Participants and Design

Our research utilised 1,020 participants (M = 30.8 years, SD = 12.1, range 17–71 years) who each completed four lineups that involved: Viewing a target person, completing a brief distractor task, and responding to an eight-person lineup. Most participants were female (n = 793, 77.7%) and Caucasian (n = 777, 76.2%), with nine (0.9%) participants not providing their age, gender and ethnicity. Just over half of participants (n = 533, 52.2%) were undergraduate students recruited via university research participation schemes at the first two authors' institutions. The remaining participants (n=487, 47.8%) were community members, recruited via social media (Facebook, LinkedIn and Twitter), email invitation, posters, and word of mouth.

During the first author's PhD, we manipulated five variables of interest using a mixed between-within participants design (see Jordan, 2021, Chapter 3). Two variables were manipulated between participants: Recognition approach (identification, confidence, similarity) and procedure (simultaneous, sequential). The other three variables were manipulated within-participants: Target appearance (no-change, change), position (early, late), and target presence (present, absent). For this book, we focus on the variables of greatest theoretical and applied interest (i.e., recognition approach, target appearance, and target presence) to enable and increase the statistical robustness of additional inferential analyses. This was deemed appropriate because the effects of procedure and position were limited and did not impact the main effect of appearance (see Jordan, 2021, Chapters 4–6).

Regarding the variables of interest in this book, recognition approach was manipulated so that participants made identification decisions with associated post-decisional confidence ratings (n = 350), confidence judgements (n = 314), or similarity judgements (n = 356). Target appearance was manipulated so that the targets' appearance changed or did not change, and target presence was manipulated so that the target was present or absent from the lineup. When the target was absent from the lineup, a replacement was included in the lineup in their place (see Jordan, 2021, Chapter 3).

Materials

As mentioned previously, participants in this research completed four lineups. To accommodate this, we selected photographs of four target persons, and eight lineup members (including a replacement and seven foils) for each target. All target and lineup photographs were sourced from the multi-PIE face database (multi-PIE; Gross et al., 2010), which comprises high-resolution passport-style images (i.e., head and shoulders) of more than 200 people, taken on up to four occasions over a six-month period. Multi-PIE was uniquely suited to our aims, as it enabled us to examine the influence of naturalistic appearance change in lineup-based recognition contexts.

For each of the four targets (all of whom were Caucasian and male), we selected three different photographs from multi-PIE to be used in the lineups. Importantly, we presented participants with one of two of these photographs during encoding (i.e., the target stimulus photograph), depending on the appearance condition (i.e., no-change, change). We then presented participants with the third target photograph during retrieval (i.e., the target photograph included in the lineup), which remained the same regardless of the appearance condition (in target-present lineups only). In no-change conditions, the target stimulus photograph and the target photograph included in the lineup were taken on the same day, so only differed in relation to one contextual characteristic (photograph background). In change conditions, by comparison, the target stimulus photograph and the target photograph included in the lineup were taken on different days and differed in relation to three person-specific characteristics (target facial hair presence, target cranial hair length, and target clothing) and one contextual characteristic. To view a visual example of our appearance manipulation, please refer to Jordan et al. (2025) Supplementary Materials.

The eight lineup members (a replacement and seven foils) for each experimental lineup were selected from multi-PIE using a resemblance-match method (see Tunnicliff & Clark, 2000). To achieve this, we grouped all Caucasian male individuals according to their approximate age and hair colour. From each group, we then selected 15 faces for each target, based on their resemblance to the target's no-change photograph. Finally, we asked 34 participants to select and rank the eight faces from each group that best resembled the respective target. The eight faces (not including the target) with the highest pooled average resemblance rankings were chosen as lineup members for each target. Of these, the lineup member with the highest average resemblance rank in each group was selected as the replacement for each target-absent lineup (see Jordan, 2021, Chapter 3). For more information relating to the construction and evaluation of lineups, including measures of defendant bias (Malpass, 1981) and Tredoux's effective size (Tredoux, 1998, 1999) for each target-present and -absent lineup, please refer to Jordan et al. (2025) Supplemental Materials.

Procedure

Regarding the experimental procedure, we directed participants to an online survey, hosted by Qualtrics XM, where they were presented with an information letter and consent form. We then randomly assigned them to one of the three recognition approaches – identification, confidence, and similarity – where participants completed the four lineups. We informed participants that target persons may or may not be included in the photographic lineups, and that, if included, their appearance and/or clothing may have changed. During each lineup, we asked participants to view a target person for three seconds, engage in a brief distractor task (i.e., watch a two-to-three-minute video and answer a related question), and make a decision or judgements from a photographic lineup.

In the identification condition, we asked participants to make an identification decision and provide a post-decisional confidence rating for each photographic lineup. To record a positive identification, participants selected the lineup member they believed to be the target. To make a non-identification, participants indicated that the target person was "not present". Directly following a decision (identification or non-identification), we asked participants to rate their confidence in the accuracy of their decision via a 6-point scale ranging from 1 (uncertain) to 6 (absolutely certain). For the purpose of analysis, this scale was recoded so that it ranged from 0 to 5.

In the confidence and similarity conditions, we asked participants to make judgements regarding every lineup member included in each photographic lineup. In the confidence condition, these judgements related to how certain they were that each member of the lineup was the target, via an 11-point scale ranging from 0 (absolutely certain that the lineup member was not the target) to 10 (absolutely certain that the lineup member was the target). In the similarity condition, these judgements related to how similar they believed each face presented in a lineup was to the target, via an 11-point scale ranging from 0 (highly dissimilar) to 10 (highly similar). For information relating to the assumptions underpinning the scale items and their limitations, please refer to Chapter 3 of Jordan (2021).

Having completed the four lineups (the order of which was randomised), we asked participants to provide some basic demographic information (age, gender, and ethnicity). Finally, we thanked participants for completing the study and presented them with a debrief statement.

Summary

In this chapter, we considered the role of appearance in recognition contexts and outlined the methodological approach to our research. We highlighted the influence of target appearance on recognition and explained its relevance when examining the theoretical and practical utility of traditional and alternative approaches to obtaining eyewitness evidence from lineups. We also provided information regarding the participants, design, materials, and procedure of our research. In Chapter 4, we present the first series of empirical findings, addressing our first research aim: To explore the relationship between identity, confidence, and similarity in lineup-based recognition tasks.

References

Baddeley, A. D., & Woodhead, M. (1982). Depth of processing, context, and face recognition. *Canadian Journal of Psychology*, *36*(2), 148–164. https://doi.org/10.1037/h0080635

Baranski, J. V., & Petrusic, W. M. (2001). Testing architectures of the decision-confidence relation. *Canadian Journal of Experimental Psychology/*

Revue Canadienne de Psychologie Expérimentale, *55*(3), 195–206. https://doi.org/10.1037/h0087366

Bruce, V. (1982). Changing faces: Visual and non-visual coding processes in face recognition. *British Journal of Psychology*, *73*(1), 105–116. https://doi.org/10.1111/j.2044-8295.1982.tb01795.x

Bruce, V., Valentine, T., & Baddeley, A. (1987). The basis of the 3/4 view advantage in face recognition. *Applied Cognitive Psychology*, *1*(2), 109–120. https://doi.org/10.1002/acp.2350010204

Charman, S. D., & Wells, G. L. (2007). Eyewitness lineups: Is the appearance-change instruction a good idea? *Law and Human Behaviour*, *31*, 3–22. https://doi.org/10.1007/s10979-006-9006-3

Charman, S. D., & Wells, G. L. (2012). The moderating effects of ecphoric experience on post-identification feedback: A critical test of the cues-based inference conceptualisation. *Applied Cognitive Psychology*, *26*(2), 243–250. https://doi.org/10.1002/acp.1815

Charman, S. D., Shambaugh, L. J., Cahill, B. S., & Molinaro, P. F. (2022). The ability to infer witness accuracy from high-confidence lineup identifications is undermined by the appearance-change instruction and target appearance change. *Psychology, Public Policy, and Law*, *28*(4), 491–504. https://doi.org/10.1037/law0000368

Chung, M., & Thomson, D. M. (1995). Development of face recognition. *British Journal of Psychology*, *86*(1), 55–87. https://doi.org/10.1111/j.2044-8295.1995.tb02546.x

Clark, S. E. (2011). Blackstone and the balance of eyewitness identification evidence. *Albany Law Review*, *74*(3), 1105. Retrieved from http://www.heinonline.org.ezproxy.ecu.edu.au/HOL/Page?public=false&handle=hein.journals/albany74&page=1105&collection=journals

Clark, S. E., & Godfrey, R. (2009). Eyewitness identification evidence and innocence risk. *Psychonomic Bulletin & Review*, *16*, 22–42. https://doi.org/10.3758/pbr.16.1.22

Criss, A. (2006). The consequences of differentiation in episodic memory: Similarity and the strength-based mirror effect. *Journal of Memory and Language*, *55*(4), 461–478. https://doi.org/10.1016/j.jml.2006.08.003

Cutler, B. L., Penrod, S. D., & Martens, T. K. (1987). Improving the reliability of eyewitness identification: Putting context into context. *Journal of Applied Psychology*, *72*, 629–637. https://doi.org/10.1037/0021-9010.72.4.629

Davies, G., & Flin, R. (1984). The man behind the mask–disguise and face recognition. *Human Learning: Journal of Practical Research & Applications*, *3*, 83–95.

Diamond, R., & Carey, S. (1977). Developmental changes in the representation of faces. *Journal of Experimental Child Psychology*, *23*(1), 1–22. https://doi.org/10.1016/0022-0965(77)90069-8

Erickson, W. B., Lampinen, J. M., Frowd, C. D., & Mahoney, G. (2017). When age-progressed images are unreliable: The roles of external features and age range. *Science and Justice*, *57*, 136–143. https://doi.org/10.1016/j.scijus.2016.11.006

Gronlund, S. D., Carlson, C. A., Dailey, S. B., & Goodsell, C. A. (2009). Robustness of the sequential lineup advantage. *Journal of Experimental Psychology*, *15*, 140–152. https://doi.org/10.1037/a0015082

Gross, R., Matthews, I., Cohn, J., Kanade, T., & Baker, S. (2010). Multi-PIE. *Proceedings of the International Conference on Automatic Face and Gesture Recognition. IEEE International Conference on Automatic Face & Gesture Recognition*, *28*, 807–813. https://doi.org/10.1016/j.imavis.2009.08.002

Hope, L., & Sauer, J. D. (2014). Eyewitness memory and mistaken identifications. In M. Yves (Ed.), *Investigative interviewing: The essentials* (pp. 97–124). Carswell.

Jordan, D. T. (2021). *Identity: A crisis of confidence? Or is it resemblance? An exploration of the different approaches by which eyewitness evidence can be obtained from lineups*. [Doctoral thesis, Edith Cowan University]. Research Online Institutional Repository https://ro.ecu.edu.au/theses/2449

Jordan, D. T., Scott, A. J., & Thomson, D. M. (2024, July 10). Think you could pick a criminal suspect out of a lineup? If they've shaved or changed their clothes, you'd probably fail. *The Conversation*. Retrieved from https://theconversation.com/think-you-could-pick-a-criminal-suspect-out-of-a-lineup-if-theyve-shaved-or-changed-their-clothes-youd-probably-fail-233117

Jordan, D. T., Scott, A. J., & Thomson, D. M. (2025). Appearances can be deceiving: How naturalistic changes to target appearance impact on lineup-based decision making. *Psychology, Crime & Law*, *31*(4), 1–28. https://doi.org/10.1080/1068316X.2023.2243001

Lander, K., & Bruce, V. (2003). The role of motion in learning new faces. *Visual Cognition 10*, 897–912. https://doi.org/10.1080/13506280344000149

Lee, J. (2019). *Facial identification: A meta-analysis of 50 years of research*. [Doctoral thesis, City University of New York]. Research Online Institutional Repository https://academicworks.cuny.edu/cgi/viewcontent.cgi?article=4455&context=gc_etds

Macrae, C., & Lewis, H. (2002). Do I know you? Processing orientation and face recognition. *Psychological Science*, *13*(2), 194–196. https://doi.org/10.1111/1467-9280.00436

Malpass, R. S. (1981). Effective size and defendant bias in eyewitness identification lineups. *Law and Human Behaviour*, *5*, 299–309. http://doi.org/10.1007/BF01044945

Manley, K. D., Chan, J. C. K., Wells, G. L. (2021). Improving face identification accuracy of mask wearing individuals. *Cognitive Research: Principles and Implications*, *28*, 27. https://doi.org/10.1186/s41235-022-00369-7

Mansour, J. K., Beaudry, J. L., Bertrand, M. I., Kalmet, N., Melsom, E. I., & Lindsay, R. C. L. (2020). Impact of disguise on identification decision and confidence with simultaneous and sequential lineups. *Law and Human Behavior*, *36*, 513–526. https://doi.org/10.1037/h0093937

Maurer, D., Le Grand, R., & Mondloch, C. (2002). The many faces of configural processing. *Trends in Cognitive Sciences*, *6*(6), 255–260. https://doi.org/10.1016/S1364-6613(02)01903-4

McKelvie, S. (1991). Effects of processing strategy and transformation on recognition memory for photographs of faces. *Bulletin of the Psychonomic Society*, *29*, 98–100. https://doi.org/10.3758/BF03335205

Memon, A., & Gabbert, F. (2003). Unravelling the effects of sequential presentation in culprit-present lineups. *Applied Cognitive Psychology*, *17*, 703–714. https://doi.org/10.1002/acp.909

Molinaro, P. F., Arndorfer, A., & Charman, S. D. (2013). Appearance-change instruction effects on eyewitness lineup identification accuracy are not moderated by amount of appearance change. *Law and Human Behavior*, *37*(6), 432–440. https://doi.org/10.1037/lhb0000049

Nakabayashi, K., & Liu, C. (2014). Development of holistic and featural processing in face recognition. *Frontiers in Human Neuroscience*, *8*, 831. https://doi.org/10.3389/fnhum.2014.00831

Navon, D. (1977). Forest before the trees: The precedence of global features in visual perception. *Cognitive Psychology*, *9*, 353–383. https://doi.org/10.1016/0010-0285(77)90012-3

O'Rourke, T. E., Penrod, S. D., Cutler, B. L., & Stuve, T. E. (1989). The external validity of eyewitness identification research: Generalising across subject populations. *Law and Human Behavior*, *13*, 385–395. https://doi.org/10.1007/BF01056410

Palu. A., Raidvee, A., Murnikov, V., & Kask, K. (2023). The effect of surgical masks on identification decisions from masked and unmasked lineups. *Psychiatry, Psychology, and Law*, 31(2). https://doi.org/10.1080/13218719.2023.2242435

Perfect, T. (2003). Local processing BIAS impairs lineup performance. *Psychological Reports*, *93*(2), 393–394. https://doi.org/10.2466/pr0.2003.93.2.393

Perfect, T., Dennis, I., & Snell, A. (2007). The effects of local and global processing orientation on eyewitness identification performance. *Memory*, *15*(7), 784–798. https://doi.org/10.1080/09658210701654627

Pozzulo, J. D., & Balfour, J. (2006). Children's and adults' eyewitness identification accuracy when a culprit changes his appearance: Comparing simultaneous and elimination lineup procedures. *Legal and Criminological Psychology*, *11*, 25–34. https://doi.org/10.1348/135532505X52626

Pozzulo, J. D., & Marciniak, S. (2006). Comparing identification procedures when the perpetrator has changed appearance. *Psychology, Crime and Law*, *12*, 429–438. https://doi.org/10.1080/10683160500050690

Righi, G., Peissig, J. J., & Tarr, M. J. (2012). Recognising disguised faces. *Journal of Visual Cognition*, *20*, 143–169. https://doi.org/10.1080/13506285.2012.654624

Sauer, J. D., Brewer, N., & Weber, N. (2008). Multiple confidence estimates as indices of eyewitness memory. *Journal of Experimental Psychology*, *137*(3), 528–547. https://doi.org/10.1037/a0012712

Sauer, J. D., Weber, N., & Brewer, N. (2012). Using ecphoric confidence ratings to discriminate seen from unseen faces: The effects of retention interval and distinctiveness. *Psychonomic Bulletin and Review*, *19*, 490–498. https://doi.org/10.3758/s13423-012-0239-5

Seitz, K. (2003). The effect of changes in clothing and posture on the development of unfamiliar person recognition. *Applied Cognitive Psychology*, *17*(7), 819–832. https://doi.org/10.1002/acp.912

Shapiro, P. N., & Penrod, S. D. (1986). Meta-analysis of facial identification studies. *Psychological Bulletin*, *100*, 139–156. https://doi.org/10.1037/0033-2909.100.2.139

Smith, A. M., Wilford, M. M., Quigley-McBride, A., & Wells, G. L. (2019). Mistaken eyewitness identification rates increase when either witnessing or testing conditions get worse. *Law and Human Behaviour*, *43*(4), 358–368. https://doi.org/10.1037/lhb0000334

Stretch, V., & Wixted, J. T. (1998). On the difference between strength-based and frequency-based mirror effects in recognition memory. *Journal of Experimental Psychology: Learning, Memory, and Cognition*, *24*(6), 1379–1396. https://doi.org/10.1037/0278-7393.24.6.1379

Terry, R. L. (1994). Effect of facial transformations on the accuracy of recognition. *Journal of Social Psychology*, *134*, 483–492. https://doi.org/10.1080/00224545.1994.9712199

Thomson, D. M. (1982). The realities of eyewitness identification. *Australian Journal of Forensic Sciences*, *14*, 150–157. https://doi.org/10.1080/00450618209411171

Thomson, D. M. (1986). Face recognition: More than a feeling of familiarity? In H. D. Ellis, M. A. Jeeves, F. Newcombe & A. Young (Eds.), *Aspects of Face Processing*. Elsevier.

Thomson, D. M. (1989). *Psychological fiction in the court room: And they did not live happily ever after. Unpublished Manuscript*. Monash University.

Thomson, D. M., Robertson, S., & Vogt, R. (1982). Person recognition: The effect of context. *Human Learning*, *1*, 497–511.

Tredoux, C. G. (1998). Statistical inference on measures of lineup fairness. *Law and Human Behavior*, *22*, 217–237. https://doi.org/10.1023/A:1025746220886

Tredoux, C. G. (1999). Statistical considerations when determining measures of lineup size and lineup bias. *Applied Cognitive Psychology*, *13*, S9–S26. https://doi.org/10.1002/(SICI)1099-0720(199911)13:1+<S9::AID-ACP634>3.0.CO;2-1

Tunnicliff, J. L., & Clark, S. E. (2000). Selecting foils for identification lineups: Matching suspects or descriptions? *Law and Human Behavior*, *24*, 231–258. https://doi.org/10.1023/A:1005463020252

Yarmey, A. (2004). Eyewitness recall and photo identification: A field experiment. *Psychology, Crime and Law*, *10*(1), 53–68. https://doi.org/10.1080/10683160210000583 79

Zwartz, M. (2016). *Identity crisis in identification evidence: Similarity judgements as an alternative to identification decisions*. [Doctoral thesis, Deakin University]. Research Online Institutional Repository. http://dro.deakin.edu.au

4 The Theoretical Relationship between Identity, Confidence, and Similarity

In this chapter, we present our first series of empirical findings and seek to address our first research aim: To explore the theoretical relationship between identity, confidence, and similarity in lineup-based recognition tasks. To achieve our aim, this chapter is divided into two sections. In the first section, we explore how non-categorical confidence and similarity judgements are distributed within lineups, and how these correspond with categorical identification decisions. In the second section, we examine how changes to target appearance between encoding and retrieval influence identification decisions (and post-decisional confidence ratings), confidence judgements, and similarity judgements. The empirical findings reported here will guide discussion in Chapter 6 regarding how confidence and similarity judgements might be positioned to address the psychological issue of identification.

Comparing Decisions and Judgements

As described in Chapter 2, theoretical accounts of recognition, such as signal detection, suggest an intuitive association between identification, confidence, and similarity in recognition tasks (Medin et al., 1995; Thomson, 1982; Van Zandt, 2000). Such theories posit that identification, confidence, and similarity all emerge from the same match-to-memory information (i.e., the degree of resemblance between a present stimulus and an individual's memory of a previously viewed stimulus; Charman & Wells, 2007; Malmberg, 2008; Tulving, 1981; Wixted, 2007), and thus, are related. Based on this theoretical understanding, some researchers have asserted that confidence serves as a direct proxy for similarity in lineup-based recognition tasks (Sauer et al., 2012), while others have argued that similarity underpins more "complex" judgements of both confidence (Fitousi, 2024) and identity (Zwartz, 2016). However, no published research has directly examined the relationship between identification decisions, confidence judgements, and similarity judgements in lineup-based

DOI: 10.4324/9781003569923-4

recognition contexts. As such, our understanding of the exact nature of the relationship between the three recognition constructs remains underdeveloped (Fitousi, 2024; Fysh & Bindemann, 2023; Jordan, 2021).

In this section, we start addressing this gap in the literature by exploring how responses obtained using the three recognition approaches are distributed across lineup members in each lineup. The following three sets of descriptive analyses directly compare patterns of categorical and continuous data within each lineup. Collectively, these descriptive comparisons offer important insights into the theoretical associations between the three recognition approaches in lineup-based recognition contexts.

Positive Identifications, and Unique Max Confidence and Similarity Judgements

To start exploring the relationship between identification, confidence, and similarity, our first set of descriptive analyses examined whether the lineup member identified most often also received the highest confidence and similarity judgements most often. The dependent variables for these analyses comprised the percentage and frequency of positive identifications, unique max confidence judgements, and unique max similarity judgements. A positive identification was recorded when a lineup member was selected as the target. By comparison, a unique max judgement was recorded when a lineup member received a judgement with a higher numerical value than all other lineup members in a lineup (e.g., one lineup member received a judgement of 8, and all other lineup members received judgements of < 8). Unique max judgements represent a method of classifying continuous data (see Jordan, 2021, Chapter 3) and therefore do not provide information regarding the strength of evidence (i.e., the numerical value of a judgement) in favour of a particular lineup member. Rather, they indicate the lineup member that participants were most confident was the target (confidence approach), or who participants thought was most similar to the target (similarity approach). In this regard, unique max judgements provide a useful basis for comparison with positive identifications, because although not directly akin to each other, both should indicate which (if any) lineup member generated the strongest match-to-memory signal (Brewer et al., 2020; Jordan, 2021; Zwartz et al., 2024).

Consistent with some previous research (e.g., Zwartz, 2016), we report levels of match within each lineup as the main point of comparison. Specifically, we use levels of match to compare identification and confidence data $^{(I+C)}$, identification and similarity data $^{(I+S)}$, and confidence and similarity data $^{(C+S)}$ for each lineup. We characterised match as high, moderate, or low. High match occurred when the lineup member who received the highest percentage of responses using one recognition approach also received the highest percentage of responses using a second recognition approach. Moderate match occurred when the lineup member who received the highest percentage of responses using one recognition approach received the second highest percentage of responses using a second recognition approach. Finally, low match occurred when the lineup member who received the highest percentage of responses using one recognition approach did not receive the highest or second-highest percentage of responses using a second recognition approach.

In Tables 4.1 and 4.2, we present the percentage and frequency of positive identifications, unique max confidence and similarity judgements, and levels of match, as a function of lineup and recognition approach for each target-present and target-absent lineup member. As can be seen, levels of match were high in all 12 target-present lineups, and in 10 of the 12 target-absent lineups. When the target was present, they received the highest percentage of positive identifications as well as the highest percentage of unique max confidence and similarity judgements. When the target was absent, the same member of each respective lineup received the highest percentage of positive identifications, and unique max confidence and similarity judgements, in three of the four lineups (Lineups 1, 2, and 4). However, a different pattern was observed in Lineup 3, where the target replacement (replacement) received the highest percentage of unique max confidence and similarity judgements, but received the second highest percentage of positive identifications.

Collectively, the findings from our first set of descriptive comparisons provide evidence of a relationship between positive identifications and unique max confidence and similarity judgements. The consistently high levels of match within each lineup indicate that unique max judgements provide a relatively sensitive indication of the lineup member who generates the strongest match-to-memory signal. This pattern of findings also suggests that identification decisions, confidence judgements, and similarity judgements are all reliant to an extent on the same match-to-memory information. Such findings support prior claims that eyewitness evidence can be obtained from lineups in terms other than identity (Sauer et al., 2008; Zwartz et al., 2024). Importantly, even the application of a relatively simplistic classification system to confidence and similarity data (i.e., unique max judgements) did not disrupt the high levels of match between responses obtained using each recognition approach.

Positive Identifications, and Mean Confidence and Similarity Judgements

To further explore the relationship between identification, confidence, and similarity, our second set of descriptive analyses examined whether the lineup member identified most often also received the highest mean

Table 4.1 Percentage (frequency) of positive identifications, unique max confidence and similarity judgements, and levels of match, as a function of lineup and recognition approach for each target-present lineup member

Lineup	*Approach*	*Target*	*LM1*	*LM2*	*LM3*	*LM4*	*LM5*	*LM6*	*LM7*	*Match*
1	Identification	**74.7 (83)**	5.4 (6)	1.8 (2)	2.7 (3)	0.0 (0)	***13.5 (15)***	0.9 (1)	0.9 (1)	High-M^{I+C}
	Confidence	**74.3 (84)**	2.7 (3)	4.4 (5)	0.0 (0)	4.4 (5)	***12.4 (14)***	0.9 (1)	0.9 (1)	High-M^{I+S}
	Similarity	**62.8 (92)**	3.4 (5)	2.0 (3)	5.4 (8)	5.4 (8)	***17.6 (26)***	1.3 (2)	2.0 (3)	High-M^{C+S}
2	Identification	**50.5 (50)**	9.1 (9)	8.1 (8)	***19.2 (19)***	4.0 (4)	4.0 (4)	2.0 (2)	3.0 (3)	High-M^{I+C}
	Confidence	**48.2 (55)**	4.4 (5)	7.0 (8)	***15.8 (18)***	8.8 (10)	5.3 (6)	6.1 (7)	4.4 (5)	High-M^{I+S}
	Similarity	**44.3 (58)**	9.2 (12)	6.9 (9)	***19.8 (26)***	6.1 (8)	3.8 (5)	4.6 (6)	5.3 (7)	High-M^{C+S}
3	Identification	**85.5 (95)**	1.8 (2)	0.9 (1)	***3.6 (4)***	2.7 (3)	1.8 (2)	2.7 (3)	0.9 (1)	High-M^{I+C}
	Confidence	**85.4 (111)**	1.5 (2)	1.5 (2)	***3.1 (4)***	1.5 (2)	***3.1 (4)***	3.1 (4)	0.7 (1)	High-M^{I+S}
	Similarity	**91.4 (117)**	1.6 (2)	0.0 (0)	***2.3 (3)***	0.8 ([illegible])	0.8 (1)	***2.3 (3)***	0.8 (1)	High-M^{C+S}
4	Identification	**88.9 (112)**	***2.4 (3)***	0.0 (0)	0.8 (1)	3.2 (4)	0.8 (1)	1.6 (2)	***2.4 (3)***	High-M^{I+C}
	Confidence	**85.1 (120)**	0.7 (1)	1.4 (2)	0.0 (0)	0.7 (1)	2.8 (4)	2.8 (4)	***6.3 (9)***	High-M^{I+S}
	Similarity	**86.7 (150)**	1.7 (3)	0.0 (0)	1.1 (2)	0.6 (1)	1.1 (2)	2.9 (5)	***5.8 (10)***	High-M^{C+S}

Note: LM = lineup member. $^{I+C}$ comparison of identification and confidence data. $^{I+S}$ comparison of identification and similarity data. $^{C+S}$ comparison of confidence and similarity data. Bolded text with shaded cells indicates the lineup member who received the highest or second highest (italicised with lighter shaded cells) percentage of positive decisions and unique max judgements.

Table 4.2 Percentage (frequency) of identification decisions, unique max confidence and similarity judgements, and levels of match, as a function of lineup and recognition approach for each target-absent lineup member

Lineup	*Approach*	*Replacement*	*LM1*	*LM2*	*LM3*	*LM4*	*LM5*	*LM6*	*LM7*	*Match*
1	Identification	10.7 (6)	8.9 (5)	7.1 (4)	7.1 (4)	***12.5 (7)***	**46.4 (26)**	5.3 (3)	1.8 (1)	High-M^{I+C}
	Confidence	7.6 (7)	3.3 (3)	8.7 (8)	6.5 (6)	3.3 (3)	**50.0 (46)**	9.8 (9)	***10.9 (10)***	High-M^{I+S}
	Similarity	10.0 (13)	3.1 (4)	5.4 (7)	7.0 (9)	9.3 (12)	**40.3 (52)**	9.3 (12)	***15.5 (20)***	High-M^{C+S}
2	Identification	***18.2 (12)***	3.0 (2)	12.1 (8)	**39.4 (26)**	9.1 (6)	9.1 (6)	4.5 (3)	4.5 (3)	High-M^{I+C}
	Confidence	***20.6 (20)***	4.1 (4)	9.3 (9)	**25.8 (25)**	18.6 (18)	10.3 (10)	5.2 (5)	6.2 (6)	High-M^{I+S}
	Similarity	15.6 (20)	15.6 (20)	10.9 (14)	**24.2 (31)**	7.0 (9)	***17.2 (22)***	6.3 (8)	3.1 (4)	High-M^{C+S}
3	Identification	***17.1 (7)***	0.0 (0)	7.3 (3)	**34.1 (14)**	2.4 (1)	***17.1 (7)***	***17.1 (7)***	4.9 (2)	Mod- M^{I+C}
	Confidence	**25.0 (24)**	6.1 (6)	3.1 (3)	***22.9 (22)***	6.1 (6)	14.3 (14)	18.8 (18)	3.1 (3)	Mod- M^{I+S}
	Similarity	**23.9 (26)**	3.7 (4)	8.3 (9)	***20.2 (22)***	11.1 (12)	11.9 (13)	18.3 (20)	2.8 (3)	High- M^{C+S}
4	Identification	**39.1 (18)**	13.0 (6)	6.5 (3)	4.3 (2)	8.7 (4)	4.3 (2)	8.7 (4)	***15.2 (7)***	High-M^{I+C}
	Confidence	**36.1 (30)**	4.8 (4)	2.4 (2)	13.2 (11)	6.0 (5)	10.8 (9)	4.8 (4)	***21.7 (18)***	High-M^{I+S}
	Similarity	**40.0 (48)**	8.3 (10)	0.8 (1)	8.3 (10)	3.3 (4)	5.8 (7)	1.7 (2)	***31.7 (38)***	High-M^{C+S}

Note: LM = lineup member. $^{I+C}$ comparison of identification and confidence data. $^{I+S}$ comparison of identification and similarity data. $^{C+S}$ comparison of confidence and similarity data. Bolded text with shaded cells indicates the lineup member who received the highest or second highest (italicised with lighter shaded cells) percentage of positive decisions and unique max judgements.

confidence and similarity judgements. Unlike our first set of comparisons, our second set of analyses sought to provide a more nuanced comparison of the data by using continuous, as opposed to categorical, measures of confidence and similarity. The dependent variables for these analyses comprised the percentage and frequency of positive identifications, the mean confidence judgements for each lineup member, and the mean similarity judgements for each lineup member. In contrast to unique max judgements, mean confidence and similarity judgements provide information regarding the strength of evidence in favour of a particular lineup member. Confidence judgements were measured via an 11-point scale ranging from "0 absolutely certain is not the target" to "10 absolutely certain is the target", and similarity judgements were measured via an 11-point scale ranging from "0 highly dissimilar" to "10 highly similar".

As shown in Table 4.3, when the target was present, they were identified most frequently and received the highest mean confidence and similarity judgements in each of the four lineups. Furthermore, the lineup member identified second most frequently received the second-highest mean confidence and similarity judgements in three of the four lineups (Lineups 1, 2, and 4). By comparison, when the target was absent, the lineup member identified most frequently received the highest mean confidence and similarity judgements in three of the four lineups (Lineups 1, 2, and 4), and the highest mean similarity judgement but not the highest mean confidence judgement in one of the lineups (Lineup 3). Further, the lineup member identified second most frequently received the second highest mean confidence judgements in two of the four lineups (Lineups 2 and 4), and the second-highest mean similarity judgements in three of the four lineups (Lineups 2, 3, and 4; see Table 4.4).

Closer examination of the confidence and similarity data revealed two additional findings of interest. First, mean confidence judgements were lower than mean similarity judgements for all eight lineup members in each target-present and target-absent lineup. For example, in Lineup 1, when the target was present, mean confidence judgements ranged from 0.76 to 5.34 while mean similarity judgements ranged from 2.92 to 6.43. Second, the difference between the highest and second-highest mean confidence judgements in each target-present lineup was higher than the comparable difference between the highest and second-highest mean similarity judgements. For example, in Lineup 3, the highest and second-highest mean confidence judgements were 6.81 and 1.38, representing a difference of 5.43. By comparison, the highest and second-highest mean similarity judgements were 7.50 and 4.08, representing a difference of 3.42.

Building upon our first set of descriptive comparisons, our second set of descriptive analyses demonstrated a high level of consistency in the pattern of positive identifications, and mean confidence and similarity judgements. The data suggest that when a lineup member was perceived as

Table 4.3 Percentage (frequency) of positive identifications and mean (SD) confidence and similarity judgements, as a function of lineup and recognition approach for each target-present lineup member

Lineup	*Approach*	*Target*	*LM1*	*LM2*	*LM3*	*LM4*	*LM5*	*LM6*	*LM7*
1	Identification	**74.7 (83)**	5.4 (6)	1.8 (2)	2.7 (3)	0.0 (0)	***13.5 (15)***	0.9 (1)	0.9 (1)
	Confidence	**5.34 (4.11)**	0.78 (1.86)	0.76 (1.70)	0.78 (1.74)	1.06 (2.15)	***1.72 (2.58)***	0.88 (1.81)	0.80 (1.84)
	Similarity	**6.43 (3.32)**	2.92 (2.39)	2.97 (2.37)	3.17 (2.62)	3.29 (2.54)	***4.55 (2.74)***	3.83 (2.62)	3.68 (2.70)
2	Identification	**50.5 (50)**	9.1 (9)	8.1 (8)	***19.2 (19)***	4.0 (4)	4.0 (4)	2.0 (2)	3.0 (3)
	Confidence	**4.06 (3.82)**	1.02 (2.04)	1.09 (2.21)	***1.98 (2.80)***	1.03 (2.15)	1.25 (2.41)	1.19 (2.33)	1.15 (2.16)
	Similarity	**5.83 (3.09)**	3.39 (2.74)	3.19 (2.74)	***4.96 (2.86)***	3.72 (2.68)	3.26 (2.62)	2.93 (2.73)	3.22 (2.75)
3	Identification	**85.5 (95)**	1.8 (2)	0.9 (1)	***3.6 (4)***	2.7 (3)	1.8 (2)	2.7 (3)	0.9 (1)
	Confidence	**6.81 (3.42)**	0.80 (1.91)	0.83 (1.80)	1.27 (2.26)	0.87 (1.91)	0.91 (1.98)	***1.38 (2.48)***	0.53 (1.46)
	Similarity	**7.50 (2.80)**	2.70 (2.23)	2.75 (2.08)	3.85 (2.49)	2.68 (2.61)	3.15 (2.64)	***4.08 (2.53)***	1.86 (1.95)
4	Identification	**88.9 (112)**	***2.4 (3)***	0.0 (0)	0.8 (1)	3.2 (4)	0.8 (1)	1.6 (2)	***2.4 (3)***
	Confidence	**6.96 (3.42)**	0.70 (1.58)	0.77 (1.81)	0.82 (1.77)	0.85 (1.80)	0.90 (1.95)	0.47 (1.33)	***1.54 (2.66)***
	Similarity	**8.17 (2.31)**	3.40 (2.61)	2.22 (2.19)	3.26 (2.72)	3.36 (2.55)	2.75 (2.55)	2.74 (2.52)	***4.30 (2.87)***

Note: LM = Lineup member. Bolded text with dark shaded cells indicates the lineup member who was identified most frequently/received the highest mean judgements in each lineup. Bolded, italicised text with lighter shaded cells indicates the lineup member who was identified second most frequently/received the second highest mean judgements in each lineup.

Table 4.4 Percentage (frequency) of positive identifications and mean (SD) confidence and similarity judgements, as a function of lineup and recognition approach for each target-absent lineup

Lineup	*Approach*	*Replacement*	*LM1*	*LM2*	*LM3*	*LM4*	*LM5*	*LM6*	*LM7*
1	Identification	11.5 (6)	9.6 (5)	7.7 (4)	1.9 (1)	***13.5 (7)***	**48.1 (25)**	5.8 (3)	1.9 (1)
	Confidence	***1.44 (2.46)***	0.81 (1.88)	0.94 (1.84)	0.90 (1.76)	0.97 (2.02)	**2.77 (3.30)**	1.20 (2.22)	1.09 (2.18)
	Similarity	***3.77 (2.69)***	2.38 (2.37)	2.71 (2.70)	3.37 (2.66)	3.09 (2.70)	**4.90 (3.10)**	3.39 (2.82)	3.74 (2.97)
2	Identification	***18.8 (12)***	3.1 (2)	12.5 (8)	**39.0 (25)**	7.8 (5)	9.4 (6)	4.7 (3)	4.7 (3)
	Confidence	***2.08 (2.88)***	1.09 (1.99)	1.66 (2.74)	**3.01 (3.13)**	1.73 (2.76)	1.58 (2.54)	1.13 (2.23)	1.24 (2.31)
	Similarity	***4.19 (2.85)***	3.56 (2.77)	3.16 (2.70)	**4.99 (2.72)**	3.75 (2.58)	4.14 (2.84)	2.80 (2.47)	3.10 (2.58)
3	Identification	***17.5 (7)***	0.0 (0)	7.4 (2)	**35.0 (14)**	3.7 (1)	***17.5 (7)***	***17.5 (7)***	3.7 (1)
	Confidence	**1.91 (2.79)**	0.83 (1.96)	0.88 (1.91)	***1.89 (2.79)***	0.94 (2.10)	1.06 (2.21)	1.57 (2.44)	0.58 (1.49)
	Similarity	***3.91 (2.89)***	2.70 (2.58)	2.84 (2.56)	**4.24 (2.85)**	2.52 (2.75)	2.77 (2.78)	3.90 (2.89)	1.90 (2.18)
4	Identification	**39.5 (17)**	***14.0 (6)***	9.3 (4)	9.3 (4)	2.3 (1)	2.3 (1)	9.3 (4)	***14.0 (6)***
	Confidence	**2.91 (3.31)**	1.24 (2.22)	1.01 (1.96)	1.49 (2.58)	1.68 (2.55)	1.71 (2.63)	1.18 (2.27)	***2.08 (2.87)***
	Similarity	**4.88 (2.98)**	3.79 (2.53)	2.42 (2.31)	3.21 (2.63)	3.47 (2.52)	3.17 (2.58)	2.68 (2.43)	***4.86 (2.73)***

Note: LM = Lineup member. Bolded text with dark shaded cells indicates the lineup member who was identified most frequently/received the highest mean judgements in each lineup. Bolded, italicised text with lighter shaded cells indicates the lineup member who was identified second most frequently/received the second highest mean judgements in each lineup.

highly similar to the target (similarity approach), this often translated to higher confidence that a lineup member was the target (confidence approach), and was *more likely* to result in a positive identification (identification approach) in both target-present and target-absent lineups. Conversely, when a lineup member was perceived as less similar or somewhat dissimilar to the target (similarity approach), this often translated to higher confidence that a lineup member was not the target (confidence approach), and was *less likely* to result in a positive identification (identification approach) in both target-present and target-absent lineups. These findings support the notion that categorical identification decisions and continuous measures of confidence and similarity judgements are all informed by the same match-to-memory information, the basis of which is the visual pattern of information available at encoding and retrieval.

Despite the apparent association between recognition approaches, closer inspection of the data revealed some potential differences between continuous measures of confidence and similarity. For example, mean similarity judgements were higher than mean confidence judgements for every lineup member in all target-present and target-absent lineups. While such differences could reflect a lack of synchronicity between the confidence and similarity scale anchors, they may also highlight important differences between the underlying constructs. As mentioned earlier in this chapter, some proponents of the non-categorical confidence approach assume that confidence serves as a relatively direct proxy for ecphoric similarity (i.e., the degree to which one or more present objects match the properties of a previously studied object stored in and retrieved from memory; Tulving, 1981) in lineup-based recognition contexts (Sauer et al., 2008; Sauer et al., 2012). However, our findings potentially challenge this assumption by suggesting that the relationship between recognition constructs is more complex than previously believed.

Mean Confidence and Similarity of Max Judgements and Mean Discrepancy in Max Judgements

In recognition of some of the potential differences between confidence and similarity, our third set of descriptive analyses examined the relationship between continuous measures of confidence and similarity in greater detail. Specifically, we examined how mean confidence and mean similarity of max judgements, and mean discrepancy in max judgements, compared for each target-present and target-absent lineup. Accordingly, the dependent variables for these analyses comprised the mean confidence of max judgements, the mean similarity of max judgements, and the mean discrepancy in max confidence and similarity judgements. Confidence and similarity of max judgements refer to the numerical values attributed to the highest confidence and similarity judgements in each lineup, and

Table 4.5 Mean (SD) confidence and similarity of max judgements, and mean (SD) discrepancy in max judgements, in target-present lineups as a function of lineup and recognition approach

Lineup	*Approach*	*Max Judgements*	*Discrepancy*
1	Confidence	6.35 (3.57)	4.38 (3.78)
	Similarity	7.88 (2.22)	2.29 (1.88)
2	Confidence	6.09 (3.31)	3.75 (3.10)
	Similarity	7.57 (2.25)	2.35 (1.96)
3	Confidence	7.50 (2.88)	5.52 (3.50)
	Similarity	7.94 (2.30)	2.64 (2.00)
4	Confidence	7.49 (3.00)	5.39 (3.53)
	Similarity	8.59 (1.68)	3.10 (2.37)

incorporate both unique max judgements (i.e., when the highest confidence or similarity rating is assigned to a single lineup member) and shared max judgements (i.e., when the highest confidence or similarity rating is assigned to two or more lineup members). Conversely, discrepancy in max judgements represents the numerical difference between participants' highest and second-highest judgements in a single lineup. Given that discrepancy is a measure of the difference between judgements for multiple members of a lineup, we pool data across lineup members for these comparisons.

As shown in Table 4.5, the mean confidence of max judgements was lower than the mean similarity of max judgements in all four target-present lineups. For example, in Lineup 2, the mean value of max judgements was notably lower for confidence (M = 6.09) than similarity (M = 7.57). Mean discrepancy in max judgements, by contrast, was considerably higher for confidence than similarity in all four lineups. For example, in Lineup 1, mean discrepancy in max confidence judgements (M = 4.38) was much higher than in max similarity judgements (M = 2.29). Consistent with target-present lineups, the mean value of max judgements was lower for confidence than for similarity; and mean discrepancy in max judgements was higher for confidence than similarity in all four target-absent lineups (see Table 4.6).

Although these findings should be interpreted with caution, we believe they reinforce some of the potential differences between continuous measures of confidence and similarity. Notably, the differences in mean discrepancy in max judgements across the two recognition approaches reflect the distinct frameworks in which the confidence and similarity constructs operate. To elaborate, confidence exists within a framework of identity; that is, witnesses express their confidence or certainty that each lineup member *is* or *is not* the target. Similarity, by contrast, exists within a framework of resemblance; that is, witnesses express the degree to which each lineup member *resembles* their memory of a target. This is an

Table 4.6 Mean (SD) confidence and similarity of max judgements, and mean (SD) discrepancy in max judgements, in target-absent lineups as a function of lineup and recognition approach

Lineup	*Approach*	*Max Judgements*	*Discrepancy*
1	Confidence	4.30 (3.52)	2.53 (2.67)
	Similarity	6.95 (2.38)	2.07 (1.82)
2	Confidence	5.30 (3.35)	2.74 (2.81)
	Similarity	6.95 (2.41)	1.75 (1.38)
3	Confidence	4.18 (3.38)	2.27 (2.56)
	Similarity	6.36 (2.42)	1.84 (1.53)
4	Confidence	4.70 (3.46)	2.32 (2.58)
	Similarity	6.64 (2.33)	1.66 (1.28)

important distinction, for it directly impacts the patterns of judgements participants can make in lineup-based recognition contexts. For example, a participant who is highly certain that one member of the lineup *is* the target should logically also be highly certain that every other lineup member *is not* the target. By contrast, a participant who perceives that one member of the lineup closely resembles the target does not necessarily have to perceive that every other lineup member has little or no resemblance to the target.

It is also worth acknowledging that confidence judgements may be more heavily moderated by non-memorial decision criterion influences (e.g., decision criteria placement, administrative pressures) than similarity judgements. As discussed in Chapter 2, it has been suggested that decision criterion influences can be effectively ameliorated with non-categorical judgements because participants refrain from making a categorical decision (Sauer et al., 2008). While this argument appears to have been mostly accepted by proponents of the non-categorical confidence approach (e.g., Brewer et al., 2012; Sauer et al., 2012), a counter argument is that participants, when asked how certain they are that each member of a lineup is, or by extension, is not the target, must still *decide* whether each lineup member is in fact the target (Jordan, 2021). The confidence in this "decision" is then scaled based on the strength of memorial evidence available for or against this outcome (Baranski & Petrusic, 2001). This is not the case with similarity, whereby establishing how similar or dissimilar each lineup member is to the target does not require a decisional component (Zwartz, 2016). While this distinction may seem trivial, its implications are important. Indeed, if the two recognition constructs are differentially affected by decision criterion influences, this would align with assertions that subjective assessments of similarity precede and perhaps inform "more complex" judgements of confidence (Fitousi, 2024). This interpretation is consistent with the notion that similarity is a relatively simple *match-based comparison* process, whereas confidence, and by extension identification, are more complex *cognitive processes* that are reliant, to an extent, on match-based comparisons.

Collectively, the findings from the first three sets of analyses point to a consistent, but imperfect, relationship between responses obtained using the three recognition approaches. All three sets of descriptive comparisons provide evidence to suggest that identification decisions, confidence judgements, and similarity judgements access and rely on the same match-to-memory information. However, the latter two sets of comparisons also suggest that confidence and similarity judgements have some unique characteristics. We believe these findings support the assertion that similarity is a relatively simple match-based comparison process that exists within a framework of resemblance (Medin et al., 1993; Tversky, 1977; Tversky & Gati, 1982); and that confidence and identification are more complex cognitive processes that exist within a framework of identity (Baranski & Petrusic, 2001; Petrusic & Baranski, 2003). At the very least, these findings suggest that while all three recognition constructs are related, there is a need for caution when assuming that they function as direct proxies for one another.

Examining the Impact of Appearance on Decisions and Judgements

As described in Chapter 3, appearance is a logical factor for exploring the theoretical relationship between identity, confidence, and similarity in lineup-based recognition tasks, because changing target appearance in the interval between encoding and retrieval represents a direct manipulation of match-to-memory information (Charman & Wells, 2007; Jordan, 2021; Jordan et al., 2025). To our knowledge, no published research has examined the influence of appearance on non-categorical approaches to lineup-based recognition. Therefore, to develop novel insights into the relationship between the three recognition approaches, it is important to examine how appearance impacts identity, confidence and similarity. Our descriptive comparisons indicate that although the three recognition approaches have some unique characteristics, all appear to access and rely on match-to-memory information. Therefore, we reason that responses obtained using each recognition approach will be similarly sensitive to manipulations of appearance.

In this section, we present three sets of statistical analyses that examine how target appearance impacts patterns of identification decisions (and post-decisional confidence ratings), confidence judgements and similarity judgements. Our statistical analyses iterate on the previous descriptive comparisons in two important ways. First, we pool data across the four lineup-based recognition tasks to increase statistical power, which was considered appropriate because preliminary analyses revealed that appearance had a consistent impact on responses across all target-present and target-absent lineups. Second, we expand our analyses to consider responses across three different types of identification decisions and max confidence and similarity judgements. This expansion allows for a more complete comparison and extends prior research that only compared positive identifications and unique max judgements (e.g., Zwartz et al., 2024).

Identification Decisions and Max Confidence and Similarity Judgements

To continue exploring the relationship between identification, confidence and similarity, our first set of statistical analyses examined the impact of target appearance changes between encoding and retrieval on participants' categorical identification decisions and max confidence and similarity judgements in target-present and target-absent lineups. The dependent variables for these analyses comprised the percentage and frequency of target identifications/max judgements, replacement identifications/max judgements, foil identifications/max judgements, and non-identifications/shared max judgements. Target, replacement and foil identifications were recorded when a target, replacement or foil was selected as the target. A non-identification was recorded when no lineup member was selected as the target. Likewise, target max, replacement max and foil max judgements were recorded when the highest confidence or similarity judgement was assigned to a target, replacement or foil, and was not shared with any other lineup members. A shared max judgement was recorded when the highest confidence or similarity judgement was assigned to two or more lineup members.

In target-present lineups, target appearance was found to influence the pattern of identification decisions, $\chi^2(2, N = 700) = 88.05, p < .001$, max confidence judgements, $\chi^2(2, N = 628) = 44.35, p < .001$, and max similarity judgements, $\chi^2(2, N = 712) = 44.80, p < .001$. As shown in Table 4.7, correct target identifications were *more* frequent in no-change (65.7%)

Table 4.7 Percentage (frequency) of identification decisions, and max confidence and similarity judgements in target-present lineups, as a function of recognition approach and target appearance

Approach	*Appearance*	*Target*	*Foil*	*Non/Shared*
Identification	No change	65.7 (230)	13.1 (46)	21.1 (74)
	Change	31.4 (110)	17.4 (61)	51.1 (179)
Confidence	No change	72.0 (226)	14.3 (45)	13.7 (43)
	Change	45.9 (144)	26.4 (83)	27.7 (87)
Similarity	No change	70.8 (252)	16.0 (57)	13.2 (47)
	Change	46.1 (164)	30.1 (107)	23.9 (85)

Note: Non = Non-identifications. Shared = Shared max confidence and similarity judgements.

than in change (31.4%) conditions, and incorrect non-identifications were *less* frequent in no-change (21.1%) than in change (51.1%) conditions. Regarding confidence and similarity, correct target max judgements were *more* frequent in no-change (72.0% and 70.8%) than in change (45.9% and 46.1%) conditions, and incorrect foil max judgements were *less* frequent in no-change (14.3% and 16.0%) than in change (26.4% and 31.0%) conditions. Shared max judgements were also *less* frequent in no-change (13.7% and 13.2%) than in change (27.7% and 23.9%) conditions.

Interestingly, the pattern of findings differed for identification decisions compared to max confidence and similarity judgements. For example, the higher frequency of target identifications in no-change (65.7%) compared to change (31.4%) conditions was associated with a lower frequency of non-identifications (21.1% vs. 51.1%). By contrast, the higher frequencies of target max confidence and similarity judgements in no-change (72.0% and 70.8%) compared to change (45.9% and 46.1%) conditions were associated with lower frequencies of both foil (14.3% vs. 26.2% and 16.0% vs. 30.1%) and shared max (13.7% vs. 27.7% and 13.2% vs. 23.9%) confidence and similarity judgements.

In target-absent lineups, target appearance did not influence the pattern of identification decisions, $\chi^2(2, N = 700) = 0.71$, $p = .703$, max confidence judgements, $\chi^2(2, N = 628) = 3.33$, $p = .189$, or max similarity judgements, $\chi^2(2, N = 711) = 0.69$, $p = .710$. Nevertheless, the pattern of findings again differed for identification decisions compared to max confidence and similarity judgements (see Table 4.8). For example, non-identifications (69.1% and 71.1%) were more frequent than shared max confidence (40.8% and 42.0%) and similarity (30.7% and 32.6%) judgements in no-change and change conditions.

Our first set of statistical comparisons provides some important insights into the relationship between identification, confidence, and similarity. As expected, our findings reveal that target appearance has a

Table 4.8 Percentage (frequency) of identification decisions, and max confidence and similarity judgements in target-absent lineups, as a function of recognition approach and target appearance

Approach	*Appearance*	*Replacement*	*Foil*	*Non/Shared*
Identification	No change	6.9 (24)	24.0 (84)	69.1 (242)
	Change	5.4 (19)	23.4 (82)	71.1 (249)
Confidence	No change	15.0 (47)	44.3 (139)	40.8 (128)
	Change	10.2 (32)	47.8 (150)	42.0 (132)
Similarity	No change	15.8 (56)	53.5 (190)	30.7 (109)
	Change	13.8 (49)	53.7 (191)	32.6 (116)

Note: Non = Non-identifications. Shared = Shared max confidence and similarity judgements.

relatively uniform effect on categorical responses obtained using the three recognition approaches. Consistent with prior research on identification (Gronlund et al., 2009; Pozzulo & Balfour, 2006; Pozzulo & Marciniak, 2006), we found that when person-specific contextual cues associated with appearance were removed (i.e., facial hair) or altered (i.e., cranial hair and clothing), participants increasingly discounted the target in the lineup as being the same as, or most similar to, the target presented at encoding. In theoretical terms, these findings indicate that changed targets generate less memorial information than unchanged targets when presented as part of a lineup (Jordan et al., 2025). This is because there are fewer contextual cues available to participants that can act as reliable markers of recognition (Thomson et al., 1982). In target-absent lineups, appearance did not impact responses obtained using any of the three recognition approaches. The lack of an appearance effect can be understood by the fact that targets only appeared at encoding, so no actual *change* was made to appearance in target-absent lineups (Charman et al., 2022; Jordan et al., 2025; Pozzulo & Balfour, 2006).

These findings suggest that responses obtained using all three recognition approaches are, to a certain extent, sensitive to changes in the strength of memorial evidence. While this continues the trend of high correspondence we have observed between the three recognition approaches, there are some noticeable patterns of divergence. For example, in change conditions, lost target identifications translated to non-identifications but not foil identifications; whereas lost target max judgements, translated to both foil max and shared max judgements. These patterns of divergence suggest that there might be some underlying differences between the three recognition constructs. However, it is important to acknowledge here that there may be a methodological explanation. Not least, that max confidence and similarity judgements are not directly akin to identification decisions. Indeed, when using max confidence and similarity judgements, there is no intuitive way for participants to reject a lineup as not containing the target (Steblay & Brooks, 2021). This is because max confidence and similarity judgements indicate which (if any) lineup member generates the strongest match-to-memory signal; not whether that memory signal is strong enough to trigger a "positive identification". This distinction is important and may have implications for the practical utility of non-categorical approaches, which we discuss further in Chapter 5.

Mean Post-Decisional Confidence Ratings in Identification Decisions, and Mean Confidence and Similarity of Max Judgements

Expanding on the first set of statistical comparisons, our second set of statistical analyses provides further insights into the relationship between the three recognition approaches by examining the influence of target appearance on participants' post-decisional confidence ratings, confidence judgements, and similarity judgements in target-present and target-absent lineups. The dependent variables for these analyses comprised mean post-decisional confidence in participants' target identifications, replacement identifications, foil identifications, and non-identifications; and the mean confidence and similarity of participants' target max judgements, replacement max judgements, foil max judgements, and shared max judgements. Post-decisional confidence ratings (i.e., the certainty participants have in the accuracy of an identification decision) were measured via a 6-point scale ranging from "0 uncertain" to "5 absolutely certain"; confidence judgements were measured via an 11-point scale ranging from "0 absolutely certain is not the target" to "10 absolutely certain is the target"; and similarity judgements were measured via an 11-point scale ranging from 0 "highly dissimilar" to "10 highly similar".

In target-present lineups, appearance was found to influence the pattern of mean post-decisional confidence in identification decisions, $t(338) = 3.52$, $p < .001$, mean confidence of max judgements, $t(228) = 7.79$, $p < .001$, and mean similarity of max judgements, $t(257) = 7.55$, $p < .001$. As shown in Table 4.9, mean post-decisional confidence in target identifications was higher in no-change (M = 3.70) than in change (M = 3.20) conditions. Likewise, the mean confidence and similarity of target max judgements were higher in no-change (M = 9.05 and M = 9.32) than in change (M = 7.42 and M = 8.20) conditions.

In target-absent lineups, appearance was found to influence the pattern of mean post-decisional confidence in identification decisions, $t(489) = -3.05$, $p = .002$, and mean similarity of max judgements, $t(356) = 3.63$, $p < .001$, only. Mean post-decisional confidence in correct non-identifications was *lower* in no-change (M = 3.00) than in change (M = 3.41)

Table 4.9 Mean (SD) post-decisional confidence ratings in identification decisions, and mean (SD) confidence and similarity of max judgements, in target-present lineups as a function of recognition approach and target appearance

Approach	*Appearance*	*Decision/Max Judgement*		
		Target	*Foil*	*Non/Shared*
Identification	No change	3.70 (1.23)	2.41 (1.15)	2.50 (1.68)
	Change	3.20 (1.23)	2.31 (1.29)	2.98 (1.65)
Confidence	No change	9.05 (1.51)	6.78 (2.41)	3.09 (2.95)
	Change	7.42 (2.21)	6.60 (2.44)	2.36 (3.12)
Similarity	No change	9.32 (1.24)	7.58 (1.56)	6.15 (2.41)
	Change	8.20 (1.68)	7.59 (1.77)	5.55 (2.73)

Note: Non = Non-identifications. Shared = Shared max confidence and similarity judgements.

Table 4.10 Mean (SD) post-decisional confidence ratings in identification decisions, and mean (SD) confidence and similarity of max judgements, in target-absent lineups as a function of recognition approach and target appearance

Approach	*Appearance*	*Decision/Max Judgement*		
		Replacement	*Foil*	*Non/Shared*
Identification	No change	2.42 (1.41)	2.20 (1.18)	3.00 (1.52)
	Change	2.53 (1.17)	2.17 (1.55)	3.41 (1.45)
Confidence	No change	7.23 (2.34)	6.37 (2.31)	2.07 (2.93)
	Change	6.44 (2.75)	6.46 (2.30)	1.64 (2.68)
Similarity	No change	7.59 (1.89)	7.62 (1.70)	5.59 (2.88)
	Change	6.96 (2.02)	6.88 (2.21)	5.58 (2.66)

Note: Non = Non-identifications. Shared = Shared max confidence and similarity judgements.

conditions. Conversely, the mean similarity of foil max judgements was *higher* in no-change (M = 7.62) than in change (M = 6.88) conditions (see Table 4.10).

Our second set of statistical comparisons provides some additional insights into the relationship between the three recognition constructs. For example, our target-present findings suggest that continuous responses obtained using all three recognition approaches are sensitive to changes in the memorial experience. We found that mean post-decisional confidence ratings in correct target identifications, and the mean confidence and similarity of target max judgements, approached the upper threshold of their respective scales in no-change conditions, yet declined significantly in change conditions. In theoretical terms, lower post-decisional confidence ratings in correct target identifications could indicate that changed targets generated smaller amounts of memorial evidence, reducing the distance with which match-to-memory exceeded participants' decision criteria (i.e., a pre-set internal threshold for responding); and that unchanged targets generated much larger amounts of memorial evidence, increasing the distance with which match-to-memory exceeded participants' decision criteria. Consistent with this interpretation, the lower mean confidence and similarity of target max judgements could indicate that match-to-memory signals generated by targets were weakened when their appearance changed.

In comparison, our target-absent findings suggest that the influence of target appearance on responses obtained using the three recognition approaches was sometimes inconsistent. For example, we found that mean post-decisional confidence in correct non-identifications was *lower* in no-change conditions than in change conditions, and that the mean similarity of foil max judgements was *higher* in no-change conditions than in change conditions. These findings could indicate that participants who made non-identifications in change conditions found it easier to discount lineups as not containing the targets because foils were selected on the basis that they resembled targets presented in the no change conditions (Jordan et al., 2025). Put simply, foils appeared more similar, and thus more difficult to reject with confidence, when they shared general appearance characteristics with the encoded target (no change) than when they did not (change). However, while this explanation is intuitive, it is difficult to reconcile with other non-significant findings. For example, the mean confidence of foil max judgements did not vary as a function of appearance. Although we have previously highlighted that confidence and similarity judgements have some unique characteristics, there is no reason to believe that they would differ with respect to the influence of appearance. This is especially true when we consider that the general impact of appearance was consistent across all other comparisons involving the mean confidence and similarity of max judgments. Therefore, additional research is needed to better understand the nature of the relationships between responses obtained using the three recognition approaches, particularly in target-absent lineups.

Mean Discrepancy in Confidence and Similarity Max Judgements

To further explore the relationship between continuous measures of confidence and similarity, our third set of statistical analyses examined the influence of target appearance on discrepancy (i.e., the numerical difference between participants' highest and second-highest judgements in a single lineup) in confidence and similarity judgements for each target-present and target-absent lineup. The dependent variables for these analyses comprised mean discrepancy in max confidence judgements and mean discrepancy in max similarity judgements. Importantly, we iterate here on the previous descriptive comparisons by calculating and reporting mean discrepancy in target max judgements, replacement max judgements, foil max judgements, and shared max judgements.

In target-present lineups, target appearance influenced mean discrepancy in max confidence judgements, $t(368) = 6.01$, $p < .001$, and max similarity judgements, $t(389) = 2.64$, $p = .009$. As shown in Table 4.11, mean discrepancy in target max confidence judgements was higher in no-change (M = 7.10) than in change (M = 5.11) conditions. Likewise, mean discrepancy in target max similarity judgements was higher in no-change (M = 3.37) than in change (M = 2.80) conditions.

In target-absent lineups, target appearance did not influence mean discrepancy in either max confidence or max similarity judgements (see Table 4.12). However, it is interesting to note that the mean discrepancy in target max, replacement max, and foil max confidence judgements was almost

Table 4.11 Mean (SD) discrepancy in max judgements in target-present lineups, as a function of recognition approach and target appearance

Approach	*Appearance*	*Max Judgement*		
		Target	*Foil*	*Shared*
Confidence	No change	7.10 (3.12)	4.64 (3.18)	1.98 (2.24)
	Change	5.11 (3.08)	3.29 (2.52)	1.53 (2.37)
Similarity	No change	3.37 (2.35)	1.96 (1.95)	1.81 (1.42)
	Change	2.80 (1.98)	2.04 (1.62)	1.47 (1.29)

Table 4.12 Mean (SD) discrepancy in max judgements in target-absent lineups, as a function of recognition approach and target appearance

Approach	*Appearance*	*Max Judgement*		
		Replacement	*Foil*	*Shared*
Confidence	No change	4.04 (2.92)	3.43 (2.51)	0.99 (1.80)
	Change	3.56 (2.71)	3.50 (2.63)	0.86 (1.80)
Similarity	No change	1.80 (1.05)	2.23 (1.84)	1.45 (1.15)
	Change	1.98 (1.38)	1.87 (1.55)	1.44 (1.24)

double the mean discrepancy in target max, replacement max, and foil max similarity judgements in target-present and target-absent lineups. For example, in target-present lineups, mean discrepancy in target max confidence judgements was higher in both no-change (M = 7.10) and change (M = 5.11) conditions than mean discrepancy in target max similarity judgements (M = 3.37 and M = 2.80; see Table 4.11).

Overall, the impact of target appearance on mean discrepancy in max judgements was relatively uniform. In target-present lineups, appearance influenced mean discrepancy in target max confidence and similarity judgements, such that discrepancy was significantly higher for unchanged targets than changed targets. The findings from this set of statistical comparisons, which are the first to examine discrepancy in this manner, suggest that irrespective of the recognition approach used, changing appearance makes it more difficult for participants to distinguish between the best-matched target and foils. This explanation is consistent with our previous statistical comparisons, which indicated that unchanged targets generated significantly more memorial evidence than changed targets. That appearance did not impact mean discrepancy in any other max judgements in target-present or target-absent lineups, is also consistent with this explanation. Apart from the target, no other lineup member consistently stood out enough to generate high levels of discrepancy, irrespective of whether the target's appearance changed.

Although the impact of target appearance on mean discrepancy in max judgements was mostly consistent, the present data reaffirm some potential differences between confidence and similarity judgements. The data clearly show how mean discrepancy in target and foil max confidence judgements is higher than (i.e., almost double that of) mean discrepancy in target and foil max similarity judgements. This continued trend in mean discrepancy in max judgements reinforces the assertion we made earlier in this chapter, namely, that confidence judgements appear to exist within a framework of identity. Indeed, we believe that higher mean discrepancy in max confidence judgements reflects that participants, when presented with a confidence scale, continue to respond in relatively precise categorical terms (i.e., Yes, that is the target; No, the target is not present). By contrast, lower mean discrepancy in max similarity judgements reflects that participants, when presented with a similarity scale, respond using the full continuum for all lineup members. This is because a participant who perceives one lineup member to be highly similar to the target can also perceive another lineup member to be highly similar to the target. For this reason, we believe that similarity judgements should provide the most transparent reflection of the match-to-memory information available to witnesses when responding to lineup-based recognition tasks.

To elaborate on this position, it is important to comment on the relative ambiguity of confidence as a psychological construct. As discussed in Chapter 2, confidence has rarely been interpreted as a pure or direct measure of memory signal information (Kantner & Dobbins, 2019; Turner et al., 2011). Instead, theories of confidence processing position confidence as a measure of the distance between match-to-memory for the best matched lineup member and a decision criterion (Baranski & Petrusic, 2001; Brewer & Wells, 2006, 2011), or the distance between match-to-memory for the best-matched lineup member and match-to-memory for the alternative lineup members (Hanczakowski et al., 2021; Horry & Brewer, 2016; Turner et al., 2011; Van Zandt, 2000). Thus, while match-to-memory appears to be a central component of confidence processing, additional non-memorial factors (e.g., the placement of a participant's decision criterion and the evidence generated in favour of unselected lineup members) also have an impact (e.g., Kantner & Dobbins, 2019).

By contrast, similarity has often been interpreted as being synonymous with match-to-memory in the context of recognition (Levi & Jungman, 1995; Seelau, 1995; Tulving, 1981; Zwartz, 2016). For example, theories of similarity processing conceptualise similarity as an internal comparison process, which involves establishing the match (or mismatch) between multiple objects or items on a continuum (Kaplan and Medin, 1997; Ross, 2008; Valentine et al., 2003; Tversky, 1977; Tversky & Gati, 1982). It is important to qualify here that we are not suggesting that similarity judgements provide a "superior" measure of recognition than confidence judgements, or indeed identification decisions. In fact, previous research has suggested that higher discrepancy is often associated with increased reliability (e.g., Brewer et al., 2020). However, we believe that similarity judgements better represent, or provide a more transparent reflection of, the match-to-memory information available to witnesses when making recognition judgements.

Summary

In this chapter, we presented our first series of empirical findings that collectively explored the theoretical relationship between identity, confidence, and similarity in lineup-based recognition tasks. We reported six sets of analyses that explored the degree of correspondence between the three recognition approaches and examined how changes to target appearance between encoding and retrieval impacted patterns of responding. Collectively, our findings reveal a high degree of correspondence between identification decisions, confidence judgements, and similarity judgements, providing evidence to suggest that responses obtained using all three recognition approaches are reliant on and sensitive to the same match-to-memory information. We also observed several distinct response patterns, indicating that the three recognition approaches may not serve as direct proxies for one another.

Based on these findings, we reason that similarity judgements likely provide the most transparent reflection of the match-to-memory information on which witnesses base their lineup-based recognition responses. Indeed, because similarity judgements are not framed in terms of identity, they alone should be interpreted as a subjective assessment of the match or resemblance that exists between a witness's memory of the target and a lineup member. In this regard, we believe similarity judgements best reflect the actual capabilities of witnesses when responding to a lineup-based recognition task. With this point in mind, it is important to consider how the three recognition approaches are likely to be used and interpreted in applied settings. In Chapter 5, we present the second series of empirical findings, addressing our second research aim: To evaluate the practical utility of confidence and similarity judgements as alternatives to identification in lineup-based recognition tasks.

References

Baranski, J. V., & Petrusic, W. M. (2001). Testing architectures of the decision-confidence relation. *Canadian Journal of Experimental Psychology/Revue Canadienne de Psychologie Expérimentale*, *55*(3), 195–206. https://doi.org/10.1037/h0087366

Brewer, N., Weber, N., & Guerin, N. (2020). Police Lineups of the Future? *American Psychologist*, *75*(1), 76–91. https://doi.org/10.1037/amp0000465

Brewer, N., Weber, N., Wooton, D., & Lindsay, D. S. (2012). Identifying the bad guy in a lineup using confidence judgements under deadline pressure. *Psychological Science*, *23*(10), 1208–1214. https://doi.org/10.1177/0956797612441217

Brewer, N., & Wells, G. L. (2006). The confidence-accuracy relationship in eyewitness identification: Effects on lineup instructions, foil similarity, and target absent base rates. *Journal of Experimental Psychology*, *12*(1), 11–30. https://doi.org/10.1037/1076-898X.12.1.11

Brewer, N., & Wells, G. L. (2011). Eyewitness identification. *Current Directions in Psychological Science*, *20*(1), 24–27. https://doi.org/10.1177/0963721410389169

Charman, S. D., & Wells, G. L. (2007). Eyewitness lineups: Is the appearance-change instruction a good idea? *Law and Human Behaviour*, *31*, 3–22. https://doi.org/10.1007/s10979-006-9006-3

Charman, S. D., Shambaugh, L. J., Cahill, B. S., & Molinaro, P. F. (2022). The ability to infer witness accuracy from high-confidence lineup identifications is undermined by the appearance-change instruction and target appearance change. *Psychology, Public Policy, and Law*, *28*(4), 491–504. https://doi.org/10.1037/law0000368

Fitousi, D. (2024). A signal detection-based confidence-similarity model of face matching. *Psychological Review*, *131*(3), 625–663. https://doi.org/10.1037/rev0000435

Fysh, M. C., & Bindemann, M. (2023). Understanding face matching. *Quarterly Journal of Experimental Psychology*, *76*(4), 862–880. https://doi.org/10.1177/17470218221104476

Gronlund, S. D., Carlson, C. A., Dailey, S. B., & Goodsell, C. A. (2009). Robustness of the sequential lineup advantage. *Journal of Experimental Psychology*, *15*, 140–152. https://doi.org/10.1037/a0015082

Hanczakowski, M., Butowska, E., Beaman, C. P., Jones, D. M., & Zawadzka, K. (2021). The dissociations of confidence from accuracy in forced-choice recognition judgments. *Journal of Memory and Language*, *117*, 1–15. http://doi.org/10.1016/j.jml.2020.104189

Horry, R., & Brewer, N. (2016). How target-lure similarity shapes confidence judgments in multiple-alternative decision tasks. *Journal of Experimental Psychology: General*, *145*(12), 1615–1634. https://doi.org/10.1037/xge0000227

Jordan, D. T. (2021). *Identity: A crisis of confidence? Or is it resemblance? An exploration of the different approaches by which eyewitness evidence can be obtained from lineups*. [Doctoral thesis, Edith Cowan University]. Research Online Institutional Repository. https://ro.ecu.edu.au/theses/2449

Jordan, D. T., Scott, A. J., & Thomson, D. M. (2025). Appearances can be deceiving: How naturalistic changes to target appearance impact on lineup-based decision making. *Psychology, Crime & Law*, *31*(4), 1–28. https://doi.org/10.1080/1068316X.2023.2243001

Kantner, J., Dobbins, I. (2019). Partitioning the sources of recognition confidence: The role of individual differences. *Psychonomic Bulletin & Review*, *26*, 1317–1324. https://doi.org/10.3758/s13423-019-01586-w

Kaplan, A., & Medin, D. (1997). The coincidence effect in similarity and choice. *Memory and Cognition, 25*(4), 570–576. https://doi.org/10.3758/BF03201130

Levi, A. M., & Jungman, N. (1995). The police lineup: Basic weaknesses and radical solutions. *Criminal Justice and Behaviour, 22*(4), 347–372. https://doi.org/10.1177/0093854895022004001

Malmberg, K. (2008). Recognition memory: A review of the critical findings and an integrated theory for relating them. *Cognitive Psychology, 57*, 335–384. https://doi.org/10.1016/j.cogpsych.2008.02.004

Medin, D., Goldstone, R., & Gentner, D. (1993). Respects for similarity. *Psychological Review, 100*(2), 254–278. https://doi.org/10.1037/0033-295X.100.2.254

Medin, D., Goldstone, R., & Markman, A. (1995). Comparison and choice: Relations between similarity processes and decision processes. *Psychonomic Bulletin & Review, 2*(1), 1–19. https://doi.org/10.3758/BF03214410

Petrusic, W. M., & Baranski, J. V. (2003). Judging confidence influences decision processing in comparative judgments. *Psychonomic Bulletin & Review, 10*(1), 177–183. https://doi.org/10.3758/BF03196482

Pozzulo, J. D., & Balfour, J. (2006). Children's and adults' eyewitness identification accuracy when a culprit changes his appearance: Comparing simultaneous and elimination lineup procedures. *Legal and Criminological Psychology, 11*, 25–34. https://doi.org/10.1348/135532505X52626

Pozzulo, J. D., & Marciniak, S. (2006). Comparing identification procedures when the perpetrator has changed appearance. *Psychology, Crime and Law, 12*, 429–438. https://doi.org/10.1080/10683160500050690

Ross, S. (2008). *Processing facial similarity: Utilizing denotative and connotative information to understand facial similarity judgments*. Retrieved from ETD Collection for University of Texas.

Sauer, J. D., Brewer, N., & Weber, N. (2008). Multiple confidence estimates as indices of eyewitness memory. *Journal of Experimental Psychology, 137*(3), 528–547. https://doi.org/10.1037/a0012712

Sauer, J. D., Weber, N., & Brewer, N. (2012). Using ecphoric confidence ratings to discriminate seen from unseen faces: The effects of retention interval and distinctiveness. *Psychonomic Bulletin and Review, 19*, 490–498. https://doi.org/10.3758/s13423-012-0239-5

Seelau, E. (1995). *Ecphoric similarity and confidence judgements of eyewitnesses: Effects of extra-memorial information*. [Doctoral thesis Iowa State University]. Iowa State University Digital Repository. https://dr.lib.iastate.edu/handle/20.500.12876/64188/

Steblay, N. K., & Brooks, W. G. III. (2021). Practical concerns for investigations and courtroom: A Commentary on Brewer and Doyle (2021). *Journal of Applied Research in Memory and Cognition, 102*), 208–211. https://doi.org/10.1016/j.jarmac.2021.03.005

Thomson, D. M. (1982). The realities of eyewitness identification. *Australian Journal of Forensic Sciences, 14*, 150–157. https://doi.org/10.1080/00450618209411171

Thomson, D. M., Robertson, S., & Vogt, R. (1982). Person recognition: The effect of context. *Human Learning*, *1*, 497–511.

Tulving, E. (1981). Similarity relations in recognition. *Journal of Verbal Learning and Verbal Behaviour*, *20*, 479–496. https://doi.org/10.1016/S0022-5371(81)90129-8

Turner, B., Van Zandt, T., & Brown, S. (2011). A dynamic stimulus-driven model of signal detection. *Psychological Review*, *118*(4), 583–613. https://doi.org/10.1037/a0025191

Tversky, A. (1977). Features of similarity. *Psychological Review*, *84*(4), 327–352. https://doi.org/10.1037/0033-295X.84.4.327

Tversky, A., & Gati, I. (1982). Similarity, separability, and the triangle inequality. *Psychological Review*, *89*(2), 123–154. https://doi.org/10.1037/0033-295X.89.2.123

Valentine, T., Pickering, A. and Darling, S. (2003), Characteristics of eyewitness identification that predict the outcome of real lineups. *Applied Cognitive Psychology*, *17*, 969–993. https://doi.org/10.1002/acp.939

Van Zandt, T. (2000). ROC curves and confidence judgments in recognition memory. *Journal of Experimental Psychology: Learning, Memory, and Cognition*, *26*, 582–600. https://doi.org/10.1037//0278-7393.26.3.582

Wixted, J. T. (2007). Dual process theory and signal detection theory of recognition memory. *Psychological Review*, *114*(1), 152–176. https://doi.org/10.1037/0033-295X.114.1.152

Zwartz, M. (2016). *Identity crisis in identification evidence: Similarity judgements as an alternative to identification decisions*. [Doctoral thesis, Deakin University]. Research Online Institutional Repository. http://dro.deakin.edu.au

Zwartz, M., Thomson, D. M., & Scott, A. J. (2024). Identity crisis in eyewitness testimony: Exploring visual similarity judgments as an alternative to identification decisions. *Criminal Law Journal*, *47*(2), 93–108.

5 The Practical Utility of Confidence and Similarity as Alternatives to Identification

In this chapter, we present our second series of empirical findings and seek to address our second research aim: To evaluate the practical utility of confidence and similarity as alternatives to identification in lineup-based recognition tasks. Specifically, we seek to explore whether the confidence and similarity approaches can facilitate accurate recognition, while allowing witnesses to access additional memorial information relative to the identification approach. To achieve our aim, this chapter is divided into two sections. In the first section, we examine the discrimination accuracy (discrimination) and reliability of categorical identification decisions (and post-decisional confidence ratings), non-categorical confidence judgements, and non-categorical similarity judgements. In the second section, we explore whether the additional information unique to confidence and similarity judgements (i.e., discrepancy) can be used to enhance discrimination. Throughout this chapter, we also consider whether confidence or similarity judgements offer any improvements to response accuracy when target appearance changes between encoding and retrieval. The empirical findings reported here will guide discussion in Chapter 6 of the viability of confidence and similarity judgements in applied settings, and inform reflection on whether, and how, confidence and similarity might be positioned to address the legal issue of identification.

Comparing the Accuracy of Decisions and Judgements

As discussed in Chapter 4, our initial analyses suggested that responses obtained using the three recognition approaches are related but do not serve as direct proxies for one another. Based on these findings, we reasoned that similarity judgements likely provide the most transparent reflection of the match-to-memory information (i.e., the degree of resemblance between a present stimulus and an individual's memory of a previously viewed stimulus; Charman & Wells, 2007; Malmberg, 2008; Tulving, 1981; Wixted, 2007) on which witnesses base their lineup-based recognition

DOI: 10.4324/9781003569923-5

responses. However, even if researchers acknowledge and accept the potential theoretical advantages of similarity judgements, it is premature to suggest that they be considered viable for use in practical settings. In fact, the subject of whether non-categorical judgements, including similarity and confidence, have practical utility has become increasingly debated (see Brewer & Doyle, 2021; Colloff et al., 2021; Dodson & Garrett, 2021; Newirth, 2021; Rossmo, 2021; Smith & Ayala, 2021; Steblay & Brooks, 2021; Zwartz et al., 2024). What is clear from this body of literature is that the criminal justice system's acceptance of any alternative approach will likely be predicated on whether the responses obtained are more accurate and reliable than the traditional identification approach (Colloff et al., 2021; Dodson & Garrett, 2021).

To date, the small body of literature examining non-categorical approaches has mostly examined whether responses obtained in the form of binary confidence classifications (e.g., Brewer et al., 2012; Sauer et al., 2008) or max confidence and similarity judgements (i.e., target, replacement, foil, and shared max judgements; e.g., Brewer et al., 2020; Zwartz et al., 2024) are more accurate than identification decisions (i.e., target, replacement, foil and non-identifications) in target-present and target-absent lineups (e.g., Brewer et al., 2020; Brewer et al., 2012; Sauer et al., 2008; Zwartz et al., 2024). As described in Chapter 2, while these comparisons have generally shown that the accuracy of confidence and similarity judgements are comparable to (Zwartz et al., 2024), or better than, identification decisions (Brewer et al., 2012; Brewer et al., 2020; Sauer et al., 2008, 2012a, 2012b), several notable gaps in the literature remain (Colloff et al., 2021; Dodson & Garrett, 2021; Sauer et al., 2019a; Smith & Ayala, 2021). For example, eyewitness researchers have never compared the discrimination of lineup responses obtained using all three recognition approaches in the context of a single study. As such, we have only a limited understanding of how the accuracy of non-categorical alternative approaches, like confidence and similarity judgements, compares with each other (Jordan, 2021). Furthermore, existing research on alternative approaches to lineup-based recognition has rarely (confidence judgements), if ever (similarity judgements), compared the accuracy of responses obtained using non-categorical judgements with identification decisions *and* post-decisional confidence ratings (i.e., the certainty participants have in the accuracy of an identification decision; Smith & Ayala, 2021; Yilmaz et al., 2025). This gap in the literature is noteworthy because post-decisional confidence ratings are almost always obtained alongside identification decisions in both experimental and applied settings (Wells et al., 2020).

In this section, we seek to address both gaps in the literature by examining how responses obtained using the three recognition approaches compare with respect to two measures of practical accuracy: Discrimination and reliability. In eyewitness contexts, discrimination, which measures the group-level capacity of participants to distinguish between targets (in target-present lineups) and target replacements (in target-absent lineups; Lee & Penrod, 2019; Mickes et al., 2012); and reliability, which measures the probability that a decision or judgement made with a certain level of confidence or similarity is correct (Colloff et al., 2021; Fitousi, 2024; Mickes, 2015), can both accommodate identification decisions and post-decisional confidence ratings.

Before we progress to our first two sets of analyses, it is important to briefly acknowledge one notable practical limitation of both non-categorical approaches to lineup-based recognition. As described in Chapter 4, neither the confidence nor the similarity approach provides participants with an intuitive way to reject a lineup as not containing the target (see also Steblay & Brooks, 2021). To help contextualise this issue, consider that in Chapter 4 our findings revealed that participants made far more non-identifications than shared max judgements (i.e., when the highest confidence or similarity judgement was assigned to two or more lineup members), and far fewer target replacement (replacement) and foil identifications than replacement and foil max judgements (i.e., when the highest confidence or similarity judgement was assigned to a replacement or foil) in target-absent lineups. While this could be taken as evidence that non-categorical approaches lack practical utility, it is important to reiterate that the max judgement classification system we adopted in Chapter 4 was chosen to provide an indication of which (if any) lineup member generated the strongest match-to-memory signal, not whether that memory signal was strong enough to trigger a "positive identification". Accordingly, we recognise that in practice it is unrealistic to expect unique max judgements made at the lower end of the respective confidence and similarity scales could be interpreted as evidence of a suspect's "guilt".

To address this practical limitation, we adopted Yilmaz et al.'s (2025) system for classifying max judgements in this section. That is, we treated all unique max confidence and similarity judgements of 5 or more (i.e., the midpoint of our 0–10 scales) as akin to positive identifications; and all shared max and unique max confidence and similarity judgements less than 5, as akin to non-identifications. Therefore, a recoded target, replacement or foil max judgement was recorded when the highest confidence or similarity judgement of 5 or more was assigned to a target, replacement or foil. A recoded "shared max judgement", by comparison, was recorded when the highest confidence or similarity judgement was assigned to two or more lineup members and/or the value of this judgement was less than 5. This approach is justified, as theories of confidence and similarity processing suggest that positive identifications are more likely to occur when participants' confidence in a selected lineup member exceeds complete uncertainty (Yilmaz et al., 2025), and when participants perceive a

Table 5.1 Percentage (frequency) of identification decisions, and original and recoded max confidence and similarity judgements in target-present lineups, as a function of recognition approach and target appearance

Approach	*Appearance*	*Target*	*Foil*	*Non/Shared*
Identification	No change	65.7 (230)	13.1 (46)	21.1 (74)
	Change	31.4 (110)	17.4 (61)	51.1 (179)
Confidence (original)	No change	72.0 (226)	14.3 (45)	13.7 (43)
	Change	45.9 (144)	26.4 (83)	27.7 (87)
Confidence (recoded)	No change	71.0 (223)	11.1 (35)	17.8 (56)
	Change	41.4 (130)	22.6 (71)	36.0 (113)
Similarity (original)	No change	70.8 (252)	16.0 (57)	13.2 (47)
	Change	46.1 (164)	30.1 (107)	23.9 (85)
Similarity (recoded)	No change	69.9 (249)	15.4 (55)	14.6 (52)
	Change	44.9 (160)	27.8 (99)	27.2 (97)

Note: Non = Non-identifications. Shared = Shared max confidence and similarity judgements.

Table 5.2 Percentage (frequency) of identification decisions, and original and recoded max confidence and similarity judgements in target-absent lineups, as a function of recognition approach and target appearance

Approach	*Appearance*	*Replacement*	*Foil*	*Non/Shared*
Identification	No change	6.9 (24)	24.0 (84)	69.1 (242)
	Change	5.4 (19)	23.4 (82)	71.1 (249)
Confidence (original)	No change	15.0 (47)	44.3 (139)	40.8 (128)
	Change	10.2 (32)	47.8 (150)	42.0 (132)
Confidence (recoded)	No change	13.7 (43)	34.7 (109)	51.6 (162)
	Change	8.0 (25)	39.8 (125)	52.2 (164)
Similarity (original)	No change	15.8 (56)	53.5 (190)	30.7 (109)
	Change	13.8 (49)	53.7 (191)	32.6 (116)
Similarity (recoded)	No change	14.6 (52)	51.0 (181)	34.4 (122)
	Change	11.8 (42)	45.5 (162)	42.7 (152)

Note: Non = Non-identifications. Shared = Shared max confidence and similarity judgements.

selected lineup member to be more similar to their memory of the target than dissimilar (see Jordan, 2021, Chapter 3).

In Tables 5.1 and 5.2, we present the percentage and frequency of identification decisions, and original and recoded max judgements in target-present and target-absent lineups, as a function of recognition approach and appearance. As can be seen, the recoded max judgements produced an increased percentage of shared max judgements and a corresponding decrease in target and foil max judgements when compared to the original judgements. For example, in target-present lineups, the percentage of shared max confidence judgements in the change condition increased from 27.7% using the original classification system to 36.0%

using the recoded classification system (see Table 5.1). Likewise, in target-absent lineups, the percentage of shared max similarity judgements in the change condition increased from 32.6% using the original classification system to 42.7% using the recoded classification system (see Table 5.2). Notably, the percentage and frequency of identification decisions remained unchanged because the max judgement classification system did not apply to these data.

Discrimination of Identification Decisions, Confidence Judgements, and Similarity Judgements

As discussed in Chapter 2, eyewitness researchers have increasingly claimed that alternative approaches to identification must enhance eyewitness discrimination if they are to be considered viable by policy makers (Colloff et al., 2021; Dodson & Garrett, 2021; Smith & Ayala, 2021; Yilmaz et al., 2025). Given the relative novelty of the non-categorical confidence and similarity approaches, limited research has investigated their practical utility for discriminating correct from incorrect responses in lineup-based recognition tasks (Sauer et al., 2012a; Smith et al., 2021; Yilmaz et al., 2025). To begin addressing this gap in the literature, we used receiver operating characteristic (ROC) analysis to compare the collective capacity of participants to discriminate between targets (target-present lineups) and replacements (target-absent lineups) using each of the recognition approaches (Macmillan & Creelman, 1991; Mickes et al., 2012). ROC analysis plots rates of correct target identifications (i.e., hit rate) and incorrect replacement identifications (i.e., false alarm rate) across different levels of response bias (Mickes et al., 2012; Wixted & Mickes, 2012). In eyewitness research, response bias is typically measured using participants' confidence ratings or judgements (Mickes et al., 2024; Smith & Ayala, 2021). However, recent research in the broader field of recognition has also measured response bias using participants' similarity judgements (see Fitousi, 2024). Therefore, we treat similarity judgements as akin to post-decisional confidence ratings and confidence judgements when constructing ROC plots.

ROC plots were constructed for all three recognition approaches, with the hit rate on the y-axis and the false alarm rate on the x-axis. For identification decisions, the hit rate was the number of correct target identifications divided by the total number of target-present lineups (at each cumulative post-decisional confidence level), and the false alarm rate was the number of incorrect replacement identifications divided by the total number of target-absent lineups (at each cumulative post-decisional confidence level). For confidence and similarity judgements, the hit rate was the number of targets who received a unique max judgement of 5 or more divided by the total number of target-present lineups (at each cumulative confidence or similarity judgement level), and the false alarm rate was the number of replacements who received a unique max judgement of 5 or more divided by the total number of target-absent lineups (at each cumulative confidence or similarity judgement level). The dependent measure in ROC analysis is the partial area under the curve (pAUC; see Mickes et al., 2012), which reveals the group-level capacity of participants to accurately distinguish between targets and replacements (Mickes, 2015; Wixted & Mickes, 2012). For context, the pAUC measures the degree to which each point on the ROC plot (i.e., hit rate-false alarm rate pair) bows away from the line of chance performance (Mickes et al., 2012). The line of chance performance (i.e., diagonal dashed line) represents the area on the ROC plot at which participants were completely unable to distinguish between targets and replacements (Mickes & Gronlund, 2017).

We also performed signal detection analysis (see Carlson et al., 2021) to confirm the findings of the ROC analyses, and to assess how discrimination varied at each level of the recognition approach and appearance manipulations. Unlike ROC analysis, signal detection analysis estimates discrimination across all levels of response bias, based on a single hit-rate and false-alarm rate pair (Mickes et al., 2014). In examining recognition approach and appearance, we conducted signal detection analyses because there were insufficient identification data in the change condition to perform the necessary bootstraps for calculating and comparing pAUCs (Mickes et al., 2024). This approach was deemed appropriate because signal detection analysis offers a useful proxy for ROC analysis in lineup-based recognition tasks (Lee & Penrod, 2019) when insufficient data prevents the computation of stable ROC curves (Mickes et al., 2014). The dependent measure in signal detection analysis is d', which, like pAUC, estimates the group-level capacity of participants to accurately distinguish between targets and replacements (Carlson et al., 2021; Lee & Penrod, 2019). A d' value of 0 indicates participants' inability to distinguish targets from replacements, whereas larger values indicate participants' increased capacity to discriminate (Stanislaw & Todorov, 1999).

In Figure 5.1, we display the ROC curves for each recognition approach and for each statistical pairwise comparison. Examination of the ROC curves reveals several interesting patterns. First, the ROC curves for all three recognition approaches sit far above the line of non-discrimination, which indicates that identification decisions, confidence judgements, and similarity judgements can all be used to discriminate between correct and incorrect lineup responses. Second, the confidence and similarity curves extend over a much larger range of the ROC plot than the identification curve. This trend in the data suggests that participants using the confidence and similarity approaches made more correct and incorrect responses at the lower end of their respective scales, relative to participants using the identification approach. Third, the identification curve sat

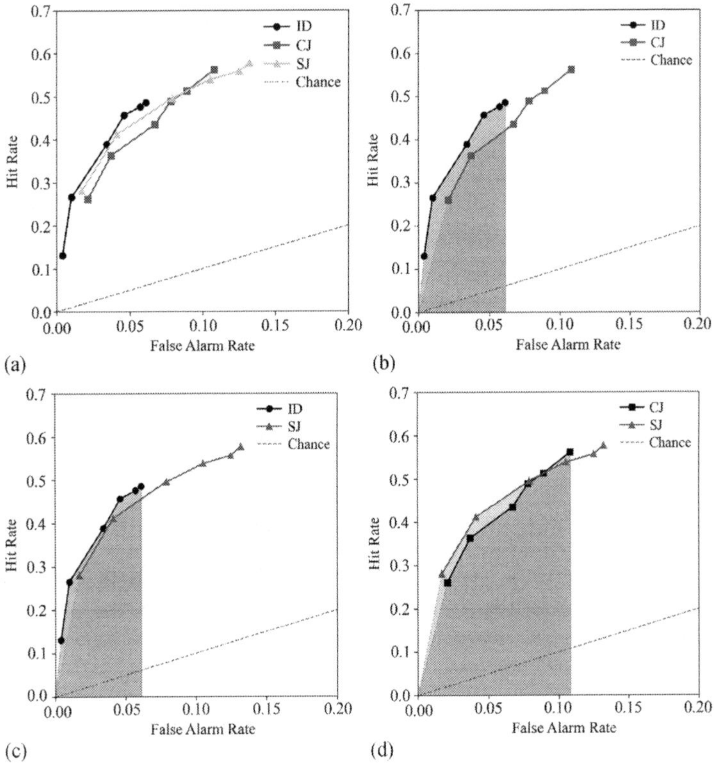

Figure 5.1 Receiver operating characteristic (ROC) curves for the three recognition approaches (Figure 5.1a), and for each statistical pairwise comparison (Figure 5.1b–d).

Note: The diagonal dashed lines in Figure 5.1a–d represent chance-level performance, and the shaded areas in Figure 5.1b–d represent the data cut-off point for each pairwise comparison.

highest in the ROC plot and did not intersect or overlap with either the confidence or similarity curves. By contrast, the confidence and similarity curves both sat slightly lower, and intersected and overlapped at different points along the x-axis (see Figure 5.1a).

To evaluate the influence of each recognition approach on discrimination, we used Z-tests to statistically compare pAUC values (see Mickes et al., 2024) and G-tests to statistically compare d' values (see Gourevitch & Galanter, 1967). Importantly, we adopted a conservative α value (= .01) for all Z- and G-tests to reduce the risk of type I errors (i.e., erroneous significant differences). We did this because we performed multiple pairwise comparisons on the same data.

As shown in Table 5.3, participants' ability to discriminate between targets and replacements was mostly unaffected by the recognition approach. Indeed, although our ROC analyses showed there was a slight visual advantage for the identification curve, the pAUC for identification decisions (.022) did not differ significantly (at $\alpha = .01$) to the pAUC for confidence (.017; $Z = 2.05$, $p = .040$; see Figure 5.1b) or similarity (.020; $Z = 0.88$, $p = .376$; see Figure 5.1c) judgements. Likewise, the pAUC for confidence judgements (.041) did not differ significantly from the pAUC for similarity (.043; $Z = 0.72$, $p = .474$; see Figure 5.1d) judgements. Furthermore, our signal detection analyses confirmed the absence of any statistically significant differences in discrimination between the three recognition approaches. Indeed, d' for identification decisions (1.51) did not significantly differ to d' for confidence (1.39; G = 0.43; p = .670) or similarity (1.30; G = 1.73, p = .084) judgements. Likewise, d' for confidence judgements did not differ significantly to d' for similarity (G = 0.80, p = .424) judgements.

Having examined the effect of recognition approach on discrimination, we also examined how appearance influenced discrimination within and across each recognition approach. As shown in Table 5.4, appearance

Table 5.3 Statistical comparisons (Z- and G-tests) of discrimination by recognition approach

Comparison	$pAUC_1$	$pAUC_2$	*Z*	*p*	d'_1	d'_2	G	*p*
ID_1 vs. CJ_2	.022	.017	2.05	.040	1.51	1.39	0.43	.670
ID_1 vs. SJ_2	.022	.020	0.88	.376	1.51	1.30	1.73	.084
CJ_1 vs. SJ_2	.041	.043	0.72	.474	1.39	1.30	0.80	.424

Note: ID = Identification decision. CJ = Confidence judgement. SJ = Similarity judgement.

Table 5.4 Statistical comparisons (G-tests) of discrimination by recognition approach and appearance

Comparison	d'_1	d'_2	G	*p*
ID, No $change_1$ vs. CJ, No $change_2$	1.89	1.65	1.42	.156
ID, No $change_1$ vs. SJ, No $change_2$	1.89	1.57	1.91	.056
CJ, No $change_1$ vs. SJ, No $change_2$	1.65	1.57	0.46	.646
ID, $Change_1$ vs. CJ, $Change_2$	1.12	1.19	0.36	.720
ID, $Change_1$ vs. SJ, $Change_2$	1.12	1.06	0.39	.699
CJ, $Change_1$ vs. SJ, $Change_2$	1.19	1.06	0.78	.433
ID, No $change_1$ vs. ID $Change_2$	1.89	1.12	4.29	.001
CJ, No $change_1$ vs. CJ, $Change_2$	1.65	1.19	2.73	.007
SJ, No $change_1$ vs. SJ, $Change_2$	1.57	1.06	3.39	.001

Note: ID = Identification decision. CJ = Confidence judgement. SJ = Similarity judgement.

had a relatively uniform, detrimental impact on discrimination for all three recognition approaches. Discrimination was significantly higher in no-change than change conditions, regardless of whether participants made identification decisions (G = 4.29, $p < .001$), confidence judgements (G = 2.73, $p = .007$), or similarity judgements (G = 3.39, $p < .001$). However, discrimination remained comparable across the three recognition approaches within both no-change and change conditions. Consistent with the previous statistical comparisons, identification decisions showed a slight, but non-significant, advantage over confidence and similarity judgements in both appearance conditions.

Our discrimination findings provide clear evidence that confidence and similarity judgements, like identification decisions, can distinguish between correct and incorrect responses in lineup-based recognition tasks. These findings align with recent research on the discrimination of confidence judgements (e.g., Smith & Ayala, 2021; Yilmaz et al., 2025) and offer initial insights into the discrimination of similarity judgements. While all three recognition approaches demonstrate the capacity to discriminate; interestingly, there was no evidence that confidence or similarity judgements enhanced discrimination relative to identification decisions. In fact, all three approaches yielded comparable levels of discrimination performance. This finding contrasts with prior claims that max confidence and similarity judgements enhance witness response accuracy by "better indexing" the degree of match between the target included in a lineup, and a participant's memory (Sauer et al., 2019a; Zwartz, 2016).

Regarding appearance, our findings suggest that neither confidence nor similarity judgements mitigate the deleterious effects of appearance change. As discussed in Chapter 3, the theoretical assumptions presented throughout this book suggest that responses obtained using the three recognition approaches should all be sensitive to the influence of appearance. This is because they rely on the same match-to-memory information (Fitousi, 2024; Jordan, 2021). Thus, a variable like appearance, that directly manipulates match-to-memory (Charman & Wells, 2007) would be expected to impair the degree to which targets can be distinguished from other lineup members (i.e., replacement and foils; Jordan et al., 2025), irrespective of the recognition approach used.

Collectively, our discrimination findings do not provide a particularly strong or compelling case for the practical utility of either confidence or similarity judgements. Indeed, researchers have increasingly claimed that alternative approaches to lineup-based recognition must enhance eyewitness discrimination if they are to be considered viable by policy makers (Colloff et al., 2021; Dodson & Garrett, 2021; Smith & Ayala, 2021; Yilmaz et al., 2025). Clark (2012a, 2012b) elaborated slightly on this position and argued that if alternatives are to replace existing practices in real-world investigations, they must, at a minimum, satisfy the "no-cost" assumption. To satisfy the no-cost assumption, an alternative approach must demonstrate that it can reduce incorrect responses in target-absent lineups without compromising correct responses in target-present lineups (Clark, 2012a, 2012b). However, our findings show, at best, that confidence and similarity judgements facilitate small increases in both correct target-present responses and incorrect target-absent responses, relative to identification decisions. This trend, which was particularly evident at lower levels of confidence and similarity, is indicative of a more liberal overall pattern of responding rather than an increase in discrimination (Colloff et al., 2017; Gronlund et al., 2012). Although this liberal pattern of responding was almost certainly driven by the requirement for participants to provide confidence and similarity judgements for each lineup member, we recognise that researchers and practitioners are unlikely to be convinced by the practical utility of non-categorical approaches that increase participants' willingness to respond, but do not enhance the accuracy of their responses (Colloff et al., 2021; Dodson & Garrett, 2021).

Reliability of Identification Decisions, Confidence Judgements, and Similarity Judgements

In establishing the practical utility of traditional and alternative approaches to lineup-based recognition, some researchers have claimed it is not just measures of discrimination that are valuable; so too are measures of reliability (e.g., Mickes, 2015; Semmler et al., 2018). While reliability is a somewhat contentious concept in the eyewitness literature (see Berkowitz et al., 2022a, 2022b; Sauer et al., 2019b), some researchers have argued that it provides the information of greatest interest to triers of fact (e.g., Mickes, 2015; Mickes & Gronlund, 2017; Wixted & Wells, 2017). This is because in practice, triers of fact are responsible for assessing the likelihood that a witness's lineup-based recognition response is accurate (Mickes & Gronlund, 2017). As described in Chapter 2, Brewer et al. (2020) initial examination of the reliability of confidence judgements found evidence to suggest that max judgements made with high confidence were often correct. However, there is still much to be learned about the reliability of responses obtained using non-categorical approaches and how these compete with the identification approach. To address this gap in the literature, we used confidence–accuracy characteristic (CAC) and similarity–accuracy characteristic (SAC) curves to examine the reliability of target and replacement identifications, and target and replacement max judgements. Consistent with our previous analyses, we also evaluated whether the reliability of responses obtained using each recognition approach was impacted by target appearance.

CAC and SAC curves provide a visual indication as to whether high confidence and high similarity are associated with high response accuracy (Mickes, 2015). For identification decisions, this is achieved by plotting the accuracy of target and replacement identifications at each specified level of post-decisional confidence. Conversely, for confidence and similarity judgements, this is achieved by plotting the accuracy of target and replacement max judgements at each specified level of confidence and similarity. Consistent with previous research (e.g., Arndorfer & Charman, 2022; Manley et al., 2021), numerical measures of confidence and similarity were collapsed (i.e., binned) into three groups, to reflect low, medium, and high confidence and similarity. For post-decisional confidence ratings, 0–2 was low, 3–4 was medium, and 5 was high. For confidence and similarity judgements, 5-7 was low, 8-9 was medium, and 10 was high. The dependent measure of CAC and SAC is the positive predictive value (PPV; see Seale-Carlisle & Mickes, 2016), which refers to the probability that the lineup member identified or who received the unique max judgement is the target (Mickes & Gronlund, 2017; Seale-Carlisle et al., 2019).

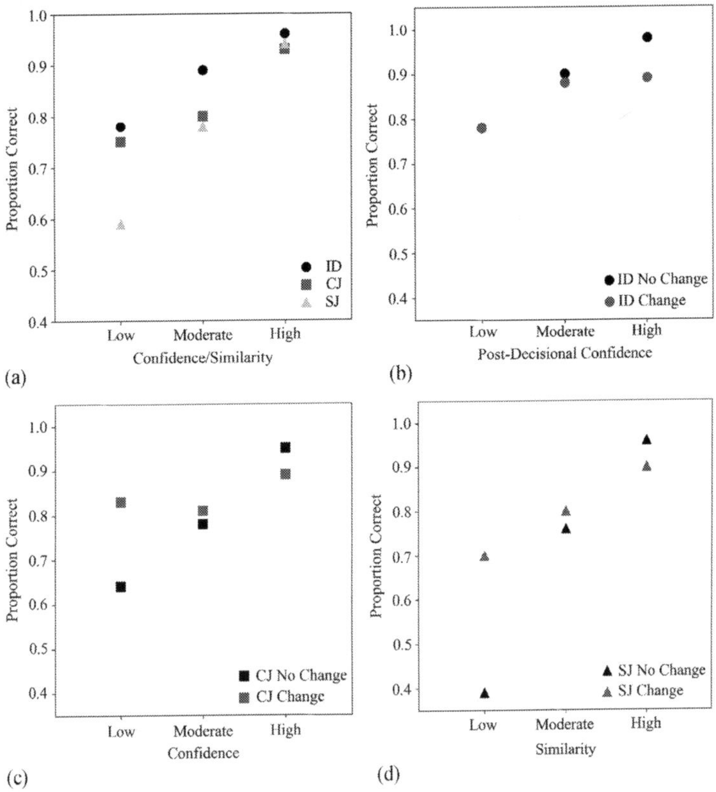

Figure 5.2 Confidence and similarity accuracy characteristic curves for the three recognition approaches (Figure 5.2a), and for each recognition approach as a function of target appearance (Figure 5.2b–d).

Note: The confidence and similarity accuracy characteristic curves were generated using the pyWitness toolkit (Mickes et al., 2024).

In Figure 5.2, we display the CAC and SAC curves for the three recognition approaches, and for each recognition approach as a function of target appearance. Examination of the curves for the three recognition approaches revealed a positive trajectory when collapsed across appearance (see Figure 5.2a). The trajectory of the curves indicated that the accuracy of responses obtained using all three recognition approaches generally increased with higher confidence and similarity. For example, the PPV (i.e., the height of the points on the y-axis) of responses made with high confidence or similarity were generally higher than the PPV of responses made with moderate or low confidence and similarity. Additionally, responses obtained using all three recognition approaches were much more likely to be accurate when associated with the highest level of confidence or similarity. For example, the proportion of target identifications made with the highest level of confidence was 0.97. Likewise, the proportion of target max judgements made with the highest level of confidence and similarity was 0.93 and 0.94.

Figure 5.2 (b–d) provides additional insights regarding reliability, as they demonstrated how target appearance impacted the relationship between post-decisional confidence ratings and identification decision accuracy; confidence and similarity and max judgement response accuracy. As can be seen across the three plots, the curves for each recognition approach were associated with a reasonably positive trajectory. Thus, regardless of appearance, responses made with the highest level of confidence or similarity were associated with higher PPV than responses made with moderate or low confidence and similarity. Despite this, the proportion of target identifications and max judgements made at the highest levels of confidence and similarity decreased (though remained measurably high) as a function of appearance change. For example, the proportion of target identifications was nearly 10% lower in change conditions than in no-change conditions at the highest level of post-decisional confidence. Likewise, the proportion of target max judgements was roughly 6% lower in change conditions than in no-change conditions at the highest levels of confidence and similarity.

Appearance also had a variable impact on the PPV of some responses made with low confidence and similarity. For example, the proportion of target max judgements (0.84) made with low confidence in change conditions exceeded the proportion of target max judgements made with moderate confidence in both no-change (0.78) and change (0.81) conditions (see Figure 5.2c). Moreover, the proportion of target max judgements made with low confidence and similarity was much lower in no-change (0.64, 0.40) than change (0.84, 0.70) conditions.

Our reliability findings suggest that post-decisional confidence in identification decisions, and the confidence and similarity of max judgements, can each serve as indicators of reliability in experimental contexts.

These findings are consistent with previous research examining the confidence–accuracy relationship for identification decisions (Semmler et al., 2018; Wixted & Wells, 2017), and confidence judgements (e.g., Brewer et al., 2020) and offer novel insights into the potential for similarity judgements to be diagnostic of accuracy. Indeed, we observed across all three recognition approaches that as ratings of post-decisional confidence and judgements of confidence and similarity increased, so too did the accuracy of participants' identifications and max judgements. This pattern was evident in our CAC and SAC plots, which showed that responses made with high confidence and similarity were associated with generally high levels of response accuracy. However, there was no evidence to suggest that any one recognition approach could provide meaningful reliability advantages over the others. In fact, the PPV of high-confidence and high-similarity responses remained relatively consistent across the three recognition approaches. This suggests that the reliability of identification decisions, confidence judgements, and similarity judgements is fairly comparable.

Importantly, our findings revealed that target appearance impacts the reliability of responses obtained using all three recognition approaches. Indeed, the proportion of target identification decisions and max judgements made at the highest levels of confidence and similarity all declined when appearance changed. While the declines in PPV were relatively modest, they nevertheless contribute to a worrying trend observed in recently published literature; namely, that the presence of factors outside the criminal justice system's control can weaken the confidence–accuracy relationship for identification decisions (e.g., Charman et al., 2022; Giacona et al., 2021; Jordan et al., 2025). Furthermore, our findings extend existing understanding by demonstrating, for the first time, that the confidence–accuracy and similarity–accuracy relationships for non-categorical judgements are equally susceptible to the disruptive effects of appearance change. The implications of this finding are important, for some researchers have claimed that post-decisional confidence can serve as a reliable predictor of accuracy for identification decisions obtained in real-world investigations (Semmler et al., 2018; Wixted & Mickes, 2022). However, our findings at least partially contradict this claim. Indeed, given that naturalistic appearance changes are thought to occur in almost every criminal investigation (Charman et al., 2022; Erickson et al., 2017; Jordan et al., 2025), we believe researchers must not overstate the utility of post-decisional confidence in identifications, or confidence and similarity in non-categorical judgements, for reliably predicting the response accuracy of witnesses in real-world contexts (see also, Berkowitz et al., 2022a, 2022b; Moore et al., 2024; Sauer et al., 2019b; Smith et al., 2021).

Finally, it is also important to reflect on two unexpected patterns of responding observed in our plots for confidence and similarity judgements. First, we found that the proportion of target max judgements made with low confidence and low similarity was both higher in change than no-change conditions. Second, we observed that the proportion of target max judgements made with low confidence was higher than those made with moderate confidence in change conditions. These patterns are difficult to interpret and seem at odds with our findings regarding high-confidence and high-similarity responses. Additional research is needed to identify the exact mechanism driving this pattern and whether these trends reflect differences between the recognition approaches, or if they are an artefact of the max classification system we adopted (e.g., Yilmaz et al., 2025).

Exploring the Accuracy of Discrepancy

Our initial two sets of analyses did not provide an overly compelling case for the practical utility of either confidence or similarity judgements. In fact, at best, we found that the accuracy of confidence and similarity judgements were comparable to identification decisions (and post-decisional confidence ratings). However, it is important to acknowledge at this point that much of the extant literature, and indeed our own work in this chapter, has facilitated comparisons between confidence and similarity judgements and identification decisions by converting the full pattern of judgements provided in the former into the equivalent of a categorical decision (e.g., max judgements). From a research perspective, collapsing eight judgements (i.e., a judgement for each lineup member) into a single max judgement (i.e., target, replacement, foil, shared) for each lineup is intuitive and practical (Jordan, 2021; Sauer et al., 2019a). Yet, researchers have increasingly recognised that relying entirely on max judgements for the purpose of comparison may undermine the "richness" of the data collected using non-categorical approaches (see Sauer et al., 2019a; Zwartz et al., 2024).

To this point, researchers appear to have mostly accepted that confidence and similarity judgements can elicit *more* information from lineups than identification decisions and post-decisional confidence ratings (Brewer & Doyle, 2021; Dodson & Garrett, 2021; Steblay & Brooks, 2021). However, the value of the additional memorial information elicited using confidence and similarity judgements remains unclear (Colloff et al., 2021; Dodson & Garrett, 2021). Put simply, we do not know if the available pattern of confidence and similarity judgements obtained within a lineup can be used to inform and facilitate improvements in response accuracy (Smith et al., 2024). Understandably, several researchers in recent years have sought to examine how the broader spectrum of judgements collected can be used to generate reliable information for practitioners (e.g., Brewer et al., 2020). To achieve this, researchers have mostly examined discrepancy, an element unique to non-categorical judgements.

As described in Chapter 4, discrepancy refers to the numerical difference between the max and the next-highest judgement in each lineup. Although research examining discrepancy is very much in its infancy, the initial outcomes suggest it can improve the reliability of eyewitness evidence (see Brewer et al., 2020; Zwartz et al., 2024). However, to the best of our knowledge, there is no published research exploring how discrepancy influences the discrimination of eyewitness responding. Accordingly, in this section, we seek to contribute directly to this emerging knowledge base by exploring how the discrimination of confidence and similarity judgements varies as a function of discrepancy. Consistent with the analyses presented in the previous section, we also examine whether discrimination at different discrepancy thresholds is impacted by target appearance.

Discrimination of Confidence Judgements and Similarity Judgements as a Function of Discrepancy

To explore if the discrimination of confidence and similarity judgements varies as a function of discrepancy, we conducted signal detection analyses across different thresholds of discrepancy. Specifically, we calculated the dependent measure, d', for lineups in which discrepancy was equal to 10, equal or greater than 9, equal or greater than 8, and so on, until discrepancy was equal or greater than 0 (i.e., all lineups). This approach allowed us to assess whether discrimination improved as discrepancy thresholds became more stringent. We do not report inferential statistical comparisons (i.e., G-tests) for signal detection analyses in this section. Instead, we provide a descriptive overview of how d' values vary as a function of increasing discrepancy thresholds, at each level of the recognition approach and appearance manipulations. We did this for two reasons. First, in certain conditions where discrepancy was very high, d' was calculated from a very low number of lineups, which introduced uncertainty into the precision of discrimination estimates (Stanislaw & Todorov, 1999). Second, calculating d' at each discrepancy threshold for every condition would have resulted in an excessively large number of comparisons, increasing the likelihood of type 1 errors (Field, 2018).

In Tables 5.5 and 5.6, we present the frequencies and corresponding d' values for confidence and similarity judgements as a function of discrepancy. For the discrepancy analyses, we did not apply the recoded max judgements introduced in the first section of this chapter (Yilmaz et al., 2025). Instead, we reverted to the original max judgements (see Tables 5.1 and 5.2) to preserve the full spectrum of discrepancy data. To account for the limited data obtained at high discrepancy thresholds using the similarity approach, we applied Hautus (1995) loglinear adjustment when computing d' values. The loglinear adjustment involves adding 0.5 to the

Table 5.5 Discrimination of confidence judgements as a function of discrepancy

Discrepancy	*Target*	*Foil*	*Shared*	*N*	*Replacement*	*Foil*	*Shared*	*N*	*d'*
= 10	113	8	1	122	6	14	0	20	**1.97**
≥ 9	133	10	0	143	8	22	1	31	**2.13**
≥ 8	165	13	1	179	11	30	3	44	**2.09**
≥ 7	190	20	6	216	15	41	5	61	**1.86**
≥ 6	210	22	10	242	20	49	7	76	**1.75**
≥ 5	243	37	27	307	28	87	25	140	**1.65**
≥ 4	274	44	29	347	34	110	30	174	**1.66**
≥ 3	311	59	36	406	43	146	38	227	**1.61**
≥ 2	331	86	47	464	60	214	49	323	**1.46**
≥ 1	370	128	60	558	79	289	82	450	**1.35**
≥ 0	370	128	130	628	79	289	260	628	**1.37**

Table 5.6 Discrimination of similarity judgements as a function of discrepancy

Discrepancy	*Target*	*Foil*	*Shared*	*N*	*Replacement*	*Foil*	*Shared*	*N*	*d'*
= 10	17.5	2	0	20	0.5	2	0	3	**2.12**
≥ 9	19.5	3	0	23	0.5	4	1	6	**2.41**
≥ 8	28.5	6	1	36	0.5	9	1	11	**2.50**
≥ 7	37.5	6	1	45	1.5	15	2	19	**2.38**
≥ 6	52.5	8	2	63	2.5	24	3	30	**2.35**
≥ 5	79.5	12	6	98	5.5	32	6	44	**2.03**
≥ 4	131.5	20	11	163	10.5	56	13	80	**1.99**
≥ 3	210.5	35	24	270	23.5	88	31	143	**1.75**
≥ 2	320.5	74	52	447	52.5	171	76	300	**1.51**
≥ 1	416.5	164	113	694	105.5	381	192	679	**1.27**
≥ 0	416.5	164	132	713	105.5	381	225	712	**1.26**

Note: We applied a loglinear adjustment to similarity data, to compensate for the lack of responses observed at moderate to high levels of discrepancy (Stanislaw & Todorov, 1999).

number of hits (target) and false alarms (replacement), and adding 1 to the number (N) of target-present and target-absent lineups (Stanislaw & Todorov, 1999).

As can be seen, response frequencies underlying hit rates (i.e., target max judgements) and false alarm rates (i.e., replacement max judgements) at high discrepancy thresholds varied considerably as a function of each recognition approach. For example, at the highest discrepancy threshold (discrepancy = 10), the frequency of target max judgements recorded for confidence was 113, compared to just 17 for similarity. Furthermore, at high discrepancy thresholds (discrepancy ≥8), replacement max judgements were extremely limited for confidence (n = 11) but entirely absent for similarity (n = 0). These findings suggest that participants using the similarity approach rarely, if ever, made errors when they perceived that one lineup member stood out from the rest. However, there was a trade-off; namely, relative to confidence, such high levels of discrepancy occurred infrequently using the similarity approach.

In terms of overall discrimination, we observed a reasonably positive relationship between measures of d' and discrepancy for both recognition approaches. That is, discrimination generally increased as higher discrepancy thresholds were applied. This positive trend continued up to the discrepancy threshold of ≥8, after which discrimination started to taper off slightly. A consistent finding across both recognition approaches was that discrimination was markedly higher than that observed previously for identification decisions (d' = 1.51; see Table 5.3) when discrepancy values were moderate to large (≥5). Furthermore, discrimination was extremely high for confidence and similarity judgements when discrepancy values approached the upper threshold of their respective scales (≥7). Only when thresholds were lowered to include discrepancy values as low as two did the discrimination of confidence and similarity judgements begin to converge with the discrimination of identification decisions.

In terms of discrimination and how it varied as a function of target appearance, we observed broadly consistent trends across both recognition approaches. The discrimination of confidence and similarity judgements was higher across all discrepancy thresholds in no-change conditions relative to change conditions. However, discrimination generally increased (with a few exceptions) in both appearance conditions as discrepancy thresholds increased. As shown in Tables 5.7 and 5.8, when relatively low discrepancy thresholds were applied (discrepancy ≥3 to 0), the discrimination of confidence and similarity judgements was mostly comparable to the discrimination of identification decisions previously observed in no-change and change (d' = 1.89 and d' = 1.12) conditions (see Table 5.4). However, when moderate to high discrepancy thresholds were applied (≥5), the discrimination of confidence and similarity judgements, for the most part, far exceeded identification decisions in both appearance conditions. Nevertheless, there were some notable exceptions to this pattern. Not least, the low discrimination value (d' = 0.52) observed at the highest discrepancy threshold (discrepancy = 10) for similarity judgements, in the change condition. The limited number of responses made at high discrepancy thresholds appears to have directly contributed to this somewhat counterintuitive finding. In this case, the application of the loglinear adjustment to address low-frequency cells artificially inflated the proportion of replacement max judgements recorded in target-absent lineups, thus driving down the value of d'.

Our discrepancy findings suggest that the information unique to confidence and similarity judgements can provide valuable information with potential practical utility for researchers and policymakers. Consistent with previous research that has shown high discrepancy is often

Table 5.7 Discrimination of confidence judgements as a function of discrepancy and appearance

Discrepancy	*No Change*									*Change*								
	Target	*Foil*	*Shared*	*N*	*Replacement*	*Foil*	*Shared*	*N*	*d'*	*Target*	*Foil*	*Shared*	*N*	*Replacement*	*Foil*	*Shared*	*N*	*d'*
= 10	92	2	0	94	5	6	0	11	**2.14**	21	6	1	28	1	8	0	9	**1.90**
≥ 9	107	2	0	109	5	9	0	14	**2.46**	26	8	1	35	3	13	1	17	**1.58**
≥ 8	126	4	0	130	7	14	2	23	**2.38**	39	9	1	49	4	16	1	21	**1.70**
≥ 7	140	7	1	148	10	18	3	31	**2.07**	50	13	5	68	5	23	2	30	**1.60**
≥ 6	150	8	4	162	12	22	3	37	**1.90**	60	14	6	80	8	27	4	39	**1.50**
≥ 5	166	12	10	188	19	41	11	71	**1.81**	77	25	17	119	9	46	14	69	**1.50**
≥ 4	182	13	11	206	21	53	16	90	**1.92**	92	29	18	139	13	57	14	84	**1.43**
≥ 3	202	19	14	235	28	74	20	122	**1.82**	109	40	22	171	15	72	18	105	**1.42**
≥ 2	213	34	20	267	36	101	26	163	**1.60**	118	52	27	197	24	113	23	160	**1.29**
≥ 1	226	45	25	296	47	139	46	232	**1.55**	144	83	35	262	32	150	36	218	**1.18**
≥ 0	226	45	43	314	47	139	128	314	**1.62**	144	83	87	314	32	150	132	314	**1.17**

Table 5.8 Discrimination of similarity judgements as a function of discrepancy and appearance

Discrepancy	*No Change*									*Change*								
	Target	*Foil*	*Shared*	*N*	*Replacement*	*Foil*	*Shared*	*N*	*d'*	*Target*	*Foil*	*Shared*	*N*	*Replacement*	*Foil*	*Shared*	*N*	*d'*
= 10	14.5	1	0	16	0.5	2	0	3	**2.29**	3.5	1	0	5	0.5	0	0	1	**0.52**
≥ 9	14.5	2	0	17	0.5	4	0	5	**2.33**	5.5	1	0	7	0.5	0	1	2	**1.47**
≥ 8	19.5	3	0	23	0.5	6	0	7	**2.49**	9.5	3	1	14	0.5	3	1	5	**1.75**
≥ 7	28.5	3	1	33	0.5	9	0	10	**2.74**	9.5	3	1	14	1.5	6	2	10	**1.50**
≥ 6	40.5	3	5	49	1.5	13	1	16	**2.26**	12.5	5	1	19	1.5	11	2	15	**1.69**
≥ 5	55.5	5	5	66	2.5	16	2	21	**2.18**	24.5	7	1	33	3.5	16	4	24	**1.71**
≥ 4	87.5	7	5	100	3.5	33	7	44	**2.56**	44.5	13	6	64	7.5	23	6	37	**1.34**
≥ 3	138.5	9	11	159	10.5	55	16	82	**2.27**	72.5	26	13	112	13.5	33	15	62	**1.16**
≥ 2	202.5	22	19	244	29.5	96	41	167	**1.88**	118.5	52	33	204	23.5	75	35	134	**1.14**
≥ 1	252.5	57	44	355	56.5	190	91	338	**1.52**	164.5	107	69	341	49.5	191	101	342	**1.02**
≥ 0	252.5	57	47	357	56.5	190	109	356	**1.55**	164.5	107	85	357	49.5	191	116	357	**0.99**

Note: We applied a loglinear adjustment to similarity data, to compensate for the lack of responses observed at moderate to high levels of discrepancy (Stanislaw & Todorov, 1999).

associated with greater reliability (e.g., Brewer et al., 2020; Zwartz et al., 2024), we found that the discrimination of confidence and similarity judgements generally improved with increased discrepancy. The mostly positive relationship between discrimination and discrepancy indicates that patterns of non-categorical judgements can yield meaningful information when not treated as akin to a categorical decision. In fact, our findings point to potential advantages of using discrepancy measures over relying solely on max judgements. Contrasting with the discrimination outcomes reported earlier in the chapter, the discrepancy data showed a clear trend whereby discrimination for confidence and similarity judgements often exceeded the discrimination of identification decisions, once discrepancy thresholds reached moderate to high levels. These findings support the proposition that large discrepancies between one lineup member and the others reflect strong match-to-memory signals (Brewer et al., 2012; Sauer et al., 2019a).

Importantly, the relationship between discrimination and discrepancy was found to vary as a function of target appearance. As expected, the discrimination of confidence and similarity judgements declined across all discrepancy thresholds in change conditions relative to no-change conditions. These outcomes are not surprising, given that we previously observed that changing appearance reduced how frequently targets were correctly identified and received max judgements, and greatly weakened the value of discrepancy measures (see Chapter 4). However, we also observed a strong and consistent positive relationship between discrimination and discrepancy for both recognition approaches. Specifically, as discrepancy thresholds increased for both confidence and similarity judgements, generally so too did discrimination in no-change and change conditions. Of relevance were findings showing that the discrimination of confidence and similarity judgements at moderate to high discrepancy levels exceeded the discrimination of identification decisions, irrespective of whether the target's appearance changed. These findings provide initial evidence to suggest that the non-categorical confidence and similarity approaches can outperform the identification approach in terms of discrimination, the metric of greatest importance to policymakers (Colloff et al., 2021). Moreover, this advantage appears to extend beyond optimal viewing conditions to more challenging, suboptimal conditions, such as when target appearance changes. If these findings can be replicated with larger, more robust samples, they could represent an important advance for the practical utility of non-categorical approaches to lineup-based recognition. Replication is particularly important given that appearance changes are likely to occur in most criminal investigations (Erickson et al., 2017), and to date, no known system variables have been shown to mitigate or improve discrimination when appearance changes (Charman et al., 2022; Jordan et al., 2025).

Collectively, our discrepancy findings are encouraging for proponents of non-categorical approaches to lineup-based recognition, as they suggest that the confidence and similarity approaches can facilitate meaningful improvements in discrimination when analyses are restricted to judgements made with suitably high levels of discrepancy. Indeed, when a participant perceives that one lineup member clearly stands out from the others, discrimination appears to be especially high. For both the confidence and similarity approaches, target max judgements made at high discrepancy thresholds comprised a high proportion of target-present lineups; whereas replacement max judgements at high discrepancy thresholds comprised a small proportion of target-absent lineups. In this regard, it seems that when judgements are made with suitably high discrepancy, the confidence and similarity approaches may both be capable of satisfying the no-cost assumption described earlier in the chapter (Clark, 2012a).

However, it is important to acknowledge that our analyses in this section were exploratory in nature and must be interpreted with caution. As mentioned previously, the number of lineups involving responses made at the highest discrepancy levels was extremely limited, particularly using the similarity approach. Although we applied a loglinear adjustment to address low-frequency lineups (Hautus, 1995), our small samples at high discrepancy may have led to unstable or error-prone estimates (Stanislaw & Todorov, 1999). This limitation underscores the need for additional research employing larger samples or experimental designs that promote a more even distribution of responses across discrepancy levels to determine the veracity of our findings. Future research is also needed to establish best practices for evaluating discrepancy data and consider how discrepancy can be reliably compared to lineup data with no equivalent measure, like identification decisions. In turn, this research should help to better establish the practical utility of discrepancy as a measure for improving lineup-based response accuracy.

Summary

In this chapter, we presented our second series of empirical findings that collectively evaluated the practical utility of confidence and similarity judgements as alternatives to identification decisions in lineup-based recognition tasks. We reported three sets of analyses. The first two sets compared the discrimination and reliability of identification decisions, confidence judgements, and similarity judgements. These analyses indicated that when confidence and similarity judgements are collapsed into the equivalent of a single categorical response, response accuracy is comparable to identification decisions (and post-decisional confidence ratings). The final set of analyses explored whether the discrepancy information, unique to confidence and similarity judgements, could enhance discrimination. These analyses indicated that when consideration is given to discrepancy measures, confidence and similarity approaches can enhance discrimination. Collectively, our findings provide initial evidence to suggest that confidence and similarity judgements can be used to inform and facilitate improvements in response accuracy, but only when the full pattern of judgements provided for a given lineup is preserved and considered.

While these findings are promising and should resonate with proponents of non-categorical approaches to lineup-based recognition, we are mindful not to overstate their applied importance. Given the exploratory nature of the research and the limitations of our sample, we are cautious about drawing definitive conclusions regarding the practical utility of either confidence or similarity judgements. In Chapter 6, we synthesise and discuss our main empirical findings, describe the psychological and legal implications of the research, and outline key limitations and promising avenues for future research.

References

Arndorfer, A., & Charman, S. D. (2022). Assessing the effect of eyewitness identification confidence assessment method on the confidence-accuracy relationship. *Psychology, Public Policy, and Law*, *28*(3), 414–432. https://doi.org/10.1037/law0000348

Berkowitz, S. R., Garrett, B. L., Fenn, K. M., & Loftus, E. F. (2022a). Convicting with confidence? Why we should not over-rely on eyewitness confidence. *Memory*, *30*(1), 10–15. https://doi.org/10.1080/09658211.2020.1849308

Berkowitz, S. R., Garrett, B. L., Fenn, K. M., & Loftus, E. F. (2022b). Eyewitness confidence may not be ready for the courts: A reply to Wixted et al. *Memory*, *30*(1), 75–76. https://doi.org/10.1080/09658211.2021.1952271

Brewer, N., & Doyle, J. (2021). Changing the face of police lineups: Delivering more information from witnesses. *Journal of Applied Research in Memory and Cognition*, *10*(2), 180–195. https://doi.org/10.1016/j.jarmac.2020.12.004

Brewer, N., Weber, N., & Guerin, N. (2020). Police lineups of the future? *American Psychologist*, *75*(1), 76–91. https://doi.org/10.1037/amp0000465

Brewer, N., Weber, N., Wooton, D., & Lindsay, D. S. (2012). Identifying the bad guy in a lineup using confidence judgements under deadline pressure. *Psychological Science*, *23*(10), 1208–1214. https://doi.org/10.1177/0956797612441217

Carlson, C. A., Hemby, J. A., Wooten, A. R., Jones, A. R., Lockamyeir, R. F., Carlson, M. A., Dias, J. L., & Whittington, J. E. (2021). Testing encoding specificity and the diagnostic feature-detection theory of eyewitness identification, with implications for showups, lineups, and partially disguised perpetrators. *Cognitive research: Principles and Implications*, *6*(1), 14. https://doi.org/10.1186/s41235-021-00276-3

Charman, S. D., Shambaugh, L. J., Cahill, B. S., & Molinaro, P. F. (2022). The ability to infer witness accuracy from high-confidence lineup identifications is undermined by the appearance-change instruction and target appearance change. *Psychology, Public Policy, and Law*, *28*(4), 491–504. https://doi.org/10.1037/law0000368

Charman, S. D., & Wells, G. L. (2007). Eyewitness lineups: Is the appearance-change instruction a good idea? *Law and Human Behavior*, *31*(1), 3–22. https://doi.org/10.1007/s10979-006-9006-3

Clark, S. E. (2012a). Costs and benefits of eyewitness identification reform: Psychological science and public policy. *Perspectives on Psychological Science*, *7*(3), 238–259. https://doi.org/10.1177/1745691612439584

Clark, S. E. (2012b). Eyewitness identification reform: Data, theory, and due process. *Perspectives on Psychological Science*, *7*(3), 279–283. https://doi.org/10.1177/1745691612444136

Colloff, M. F., Wilson, B. M., & Flowe, H. D. (2021). Legal system v. eyewitness: The jury is still out on who is better able to reduce eyewitness error (variance). *Journal of Applied Research in Memory and Cognition*, *10*(2), 200–204. https://doi.org/10.1016/j.jarmac.2021.04.001

Colloff, M. F., Wade, K. A., Wixted, J. T., & Maylor, E. A. (2017). A signal-detection analysis of eyewitness identification across the adult lifespan. *Psychology and Aging*, *32*(3), 243–258. https://doi.org/10.1037/pag0000168

Dodson, C. S., & Garrett, B. L. (2021). Can we get over IDs? *Journal of Applied Research in Memory and Cognition*, *10*(2), 212–214. https://doi.org/10.1016/j.jarmac.2021.03.008

Erickson, W. B., Lampinen, J. M., Frowd, C. D., & Mahoney, G. (2017). When age-progressed images are unreliable: The roles of external features and age range. *Science & Justice*, *57*(2), 136–143. https://doi.org/10.1016/j.scijus.2016.11.006

Field, A. (2018). *Discovering statistics using IBM SPSS statistics (5th ed)*. Sage.

Fitousi, D. (2024). A signal detection-based confidence-similarity model of face matching. *Psychological Review*, *131*(3), 625–663. https://doi.org/10.1037/rev0000435

Giacona, A. M., Lampinen, J. M., & Anastasi, J. S. (2021). Estimator variables can matter even for high-confidence lineup identifications made under pristine conditions. *Law and Human Behavior*, *45*, 256–270. https://doi.org/10.1037/lhb0000381

Gourevitch, V., & Galanter, E. (1967). A significance test for one parameter isosensitivity functions. *Psychometrika*, *32*(1), 25–33. https://doi.org/10.1007/BF02289402

Gronlund, S. D., Carlson, C. A., Neuschatz, J. S., Goodsell, C. A., Wetmore, S. A., Wooten, A., & Graham, M. (2012). Showups versus lineups: An evaluation using ROC analysis. *Journal of Applied Research in Memory and Cognition*, *1*(4), 221–228. https://doi.org/10.1016/j.jarmac.2012.09.003

Hautus, M. J. (1995). Corrections for extreme proportions and their biasing effects on estimated values of d′. *Behavior Research Methods, Instruments & Computers*, *27*(1), 46–51. https://doi.org/10.3758/BF03203619

Jordan, D. T. (2021). *Identity: A crisis of confidence? Or is it resemblance? An exploration of the different approaches by which eyewitness evidence can be obtained from lineups*. [Doctoral thesis, Edith Cowan University]. Research Online Institutional Repository. https://ro.ecu.edu.au/theses/2449

Jordan, D. T., Scott, A. J., & Thomson, D. M. (2025). Appearances can be deceiving: How naturalistic changes to target appearance impact on lineup-based decision making. *Psychology, Crime & Law*, *31*(4), 1–28. https://doi.org/10.1080/1068316X.2023.2243001

Lee, J., & Penrod, S. D. (2019). New signal detection theory-based framework for eyewitness performance in lineups. *Law and Human Behavior*, *43*(5), 436–454. https://doi.org/10.1037/lhb0000343

Macmillan, N., & Creelman, C. (1991). *Detection theory: A user's guide*. Cambridge University Press.

Malmberg, K. (2008). Recognition memory: A review of the critical findings and an integrated theory for relating them. *Cognitive Psychology*, *57*, 335–384. https://doi.org/10.1016/j.cogpsych.2008.02.004

Manley, K. D., Chan, J. C. K., Wells, G. L. (2021). Improving face identification accuracy of mask wearing individuals. *Cognitive Research: Principles and Implications*, *28*, 27. https://doi.org/10.1186/s41235-022-00369-7

Mickes, L. (2015). Receiver operating characteristic analysis and confidence-accuracy characteristic analysis in investigations of system variables and estimator variables that effect eyewitness memory. *Journal of Applied Research in Memory and Cognition*, *4*, 93–105. https://doi.org/10.1016/j.jarmac.2015.01.003

Mickes, L., Flowe, H. D., & Wixted, J. T. (2012). Receiver operating characteristic analysis of eyewitness memory: Comparing the diagnostic accuracy of simultaneous versus sequential lineups. *Journal of Experimental Psychology*, *18*(4), 361–376. https://doi.org/10.1037/a0030609

Mickes, L. & Gronlund, S. D. (2017). Eyewitness identification. J. H. Byrne (Ed.) *Learning and memory: A comprehensive reference 2E, Volume Cognitive Psychology of Memory*. Elsevier.

Mickes, L., Moreland, M. B., Clark, S. E., & Wixted, J. T. (2014). Missing the information needed to perform ROC analysis? Then compute d', not the diagnosticity ratio. *Journal of Applied Research in Memory and Cognition*, *3*, 58–62. https://doi.org/10.1016/j.jarmac.2014.04.007

Mickes, L., Seale-Carlisle, T. M., Chen, X., & Boogert, S. (2024). pyWitness 1.0: A python eyewitness identification analysis toolkit. *Behavior Research Methods*, *56*(3), 1533–1550. https://doi.org/10.3758/s13428-023-02108-2

Moore, K. M., Pennekamp, P., Yu, C., & Zwemer, D. U. (2024). Eyewitness confidence does not necessarily indicate identification accuracy. *Policy Insights from the Behavioral and Brain Sciences*, *11*(2), 149–155. https://doi.org/10.1177/23727322241268384

Newirth, K. A. (2021). The change to make change: A call for a moratorium on the admissibility of eyewitness identification evidence. *Journal of Applied Research in Memory and Cognition*, *10*(2), 225–228. https://doi.org/10.1016/j.jarmac.2021.05.004

Rossmo, D. K. (2021). Delivering more information to and from lineup witnesses: Commentary on Brewer and Doyle. *Journal of Applied Research in Memory and Cognition*, *10*(2), 196–199. https://doi.org/10.1016/j.jarmac.2021.03.004

Sauer, J. D., Brewer, N., & Weber, N. (2008). Multiple confidence estimates as indices of eyewitness memory. *Journal of Experimental Psychology*, *137*(3), 528–547. https://doi.org/10.1037/a0012712

Sauer, J. D., Brewer, N., & Weber, N. (2012b). Using confidence ratings to identify a target among foils. *Journal of Applied Research in Memory and Cognition*, *1*, 80–88. https://doi.org/10.1016/j.jarmac.2012.03.003

Sauer, J. D., Palmer, M. A., & Brewer, N. (2019a). Eyewitness identification. In N. Brewer & A. Douglas (Eds.), *Psychological science and the law*. Guilford Press.

Sauer, J. D., Palmer, M. A., & Brewer, N. (2019b). Pitfalls in using eyewitness confidence to diagnose the accuracy of an individual identification decision. *Psychology, Public Policy, and Law*, *25*(3), 147–165. https://doi.org/10.1037/law0000203

Sauer, J. D., Weber, N., & Brewer, N. (2012a). Using ecphoric confidence ratings to discriminate seen from unseen faces: The effects of retention interval and distinctiveness. *Psychonomic Bulletin and Review*, *19*, 490–498. https://doi.org/10.3758/s13423-012-0239-5

Seale-Carlisle, T. M., Colloff, M. F., Flowe, H. D., Wells, W., Wixted, J. T., & Mickes, L. (2019). Confidence and response time as indicators of eyewitness identification accuracy in the lab and in the real world. *Journal of Applied Research in Memory and Cognition*, *8*(4), 420–428. https://doi.org/10.1016/j.jarmac.2019.09.003

Seale-Carlisle, T. M., & Mickes, L. (2016). US lineups outperform UK lineups. *Royal Society Open Science 3*(9). https://doi.org/10.1098/rsos.160300

Semmler, C., Dunn, J., Mickes, L., & Wixted, J. T. (2018). The role of estimator variables in eyewitness identification. *Journal of Experimental Psychology: Applied*, *24*(3), 400. https://doi.org/10.1037/xap0000157

Smith, A. M., & Ayala, N. T. (2021). Do traditional lineups undermine the capacity for eyewitness memory to rule out innocent suspects? *Journal of Applied Research in Memory and Cognition*, *10*(2), 215–220. https://doi.org/10.1016/j.jarmac.2021.03.003

Smith, A. M., Smalarz, L., Ditchfield, R., & Ayala, N. T. (2021). Evaluating the claim that high confidence implies high accuracy in eyewitness identification. *Psychology, Public Policy, and Law*, *27*(4), 479–491. https://doi.org/10.1037/law0000324

Smith, A. M., Ying, R. C., Ayala, N. T., & Goldstein, A. R. (2024). The untapped potential of lineups: Using eyewitness memory to rule out innocent suspects. *Psychology, Crime & Law*, *30*(10), 1580–1590. https://doi.org/10.1080/1068316X.2023.2242998

Stanislaw, H., & Todorov, N. (1999). Calculation of signal detection theory measures. *Behavior Research Methods, Instruments & Computers, 31*(1), 137–149. https://doi.org/10.3758/BF03207704

Steblay, N. K., & Brooks, W. G. III. (2021). Practical concerns for investigations and courtroom: A commentary on Brewer and Doyle (2021). *Journal of Applied Research in Memory and Cognition, 10*(2), 208–211. https://doi.org/10.1016/j.jarmac.2021.03.005

Tulving, E. (1981). Similarity relations in recognition. *Journal of Verbal Learning and Verbal Behaviour, 20*, 479–496. https://doi.org/10.1016/S0022-5371(81)90129-8

Wells, G. L., Kovera, M. B., Douglass, A. B., Brewer, N., Meissner, C. A., & Wixted, J. T. (2020). Policy and procedure recommendations for the collection and preservation of eyewitness identification evidence. *Law and Human Behaviour, 44*(1), 3–36. https://doi.org/10.1037/lhb0000359

Wixted, J. T., & Wells, G. L. (2017). The relationship between eyewitness confidence and identification accuracy: A new synthesis. *Psychological Science in the Public Interest, 18*, 10–65. https://doi.org/10.1177/1529100616686966

Wixted, J. T. (2007). Dual process theory and signal detection theory of recognition memory. *Psychological Review, 114*(1), 152–176. https://doi.org/10.1037/0033-295X.114.1.152

Wixted, J. T. & Mickes, L. (2012). The field of eyewitness memory should abandon probative value and embrace Receiver Operating Characteristic analysis. *Perspectives on Psychological Science, 7*, 275–278. http://doi.org/10.1177/1745691612442906

Wixted, J. T., & Mickes, L. (2022). Eyewitness memory is reliable, but the criminal justice system is not. *Memory, 30*(1), 67–72. https://doi.org/10.1080/09658211.2021.1974485

Yilmaz, A. S., Wilson, B. M., & Wixted, J.T. (2025). A rate-them-all lineup procedure increases information and reduces discriminability. *Journal of Experimental Psychology: Applied, 31*(1), 1–11. https://doi.org/10.1037/xap0000524

Zwartz, M. (2016). *Identity crisis in identification evidence: Similarity judgements as an alternative to identification decisions*. [Doctoral thesis, Deakin University]. Research Online Institutional Repository. http://dro.deakin.edu.au

Zwartz, M., Thomson, D. M., & Scott, A. J. (2024). Identity crisis in eyewitness testimony: Exploring visual similarity judgments as an alternative to identification decisions. *Criminal Law Journal, 47*(2), 93–108.

6 Conclusion

In this chapter, we conclude this book by reflecting on the research findings and describing their implications for theory and practice. We synthesise and discuss the main empirical findings from Chapters 4 and 5, relating them to prior theoretical and empirical literature where appropriate, and discussing their relevance for researchers and practitioners. We then describe the broader psychological and legal implications of the research. Specifically, we revisit the psychological and legal issues of identification introduced in Chapter 1 and discuss whether the non-categorical confidence and similarity approaches are positioned to address the constraints of the enduring but flawed traditional categorical identification approach. Finally, we outline key limitations and promising avenues for future research.

Empirical Findings

The research we presented in this book sought to extend understanding of traditional and alternative approaches to lineup-based recognition by exploring how non-categorical confidence and similarity judgements correspond and compete with identification decisions and each other in lineup-based recognition tasks. Specifically, we addressed the following two research aims:

Aim 1: To explore the theoretical relationship between identification, confidence, and similarity in lineup-based recognition tasks.
Aim 2: To evaluate the practical utility of confidence and similarity judgements as alternatives to identification decisions in lineup-based recognition tasks.

To address these aims, we conducted an online survey with 1,020 participants, who each completed four lineups. Participants responded to our lineups using either identification decisions and post-decisional confidence ratings (n = 350), confidence judgements (n = 314), or similarity

DOI: 10.4324/9781003569923-6

judgements (n = 356). To build on existing knowledge, we examined the effects of two additional variables of applied and theoretical interest: target appearance and target presence.

In Chapter 4, we directly addressed the first research aim by exploring the theoretical relationship between identity, confidence, and similarity in lineup-based recognition tasks. We reported six sets of analyses that explored the degree of correspondence between the three recognition approaches and examined how changes to target appearance between encoding and retrieval impacted patterns of responding. Our first three sets of analyses revealed generally high levels of correspondence between identification decisions, confidence judgements, and similarity judgements, and how they were distributed within lineups. For example, the lineup member who received the highest percentage of positive identifications (i.e., when a lineup member is selected as the target) in the identification condition, always received either the highest (target present and absent) or second highest (target absent) percentage of unique max confidence and similarity judgements (i.e., when a lineup member receives a judgement with a higher numerical value than all other lineup members) in the confidence and similarity conditions. In addition, our second three sets of analyses showed that the impact of appearance on participant responses was fairly uniform across the three approaches. For example, the frequency with which targets were correctly identified and received max confidence and similarity judgements all experienced a similar and substantial decline when their appearance changed between encoding and retrieval.

While there is a dearth of directly relevant literature, our findings broadly align with empirical research conducted in the field of face recognition (e.g., Fitousi, 2024) that found similarity ratings exhibit high levels of correspondence with binary identification decisions and confidence ratings in face matching tasks. In combination, these findings support the assumption that the three recognition approaches access and rely on the same match-to-memory information, the basis of which is the visual pattern of information available at encoding and retrieval.

Despite the association between recognition approaches, the data revealed some interesting points of divergence, notably in continuous measures of confidence and similarity. For example, the value of mean max judgements (i.e., the average numerical value attributed to max confidence and similarity judgements) was always higher for similarity than confidence judgements, whereas the value of mean discrepancy (i.e., the average numerical difference between participants' max and second-highest judgements in a single lineup) was always higher for confidence than similarity judgements. These patterns of divergence contrast with the claims of some prior researchers, who have argued that confidence and similarity serve as direct proxies for one another in lineup-based recognition contexts (see Sauer et al., 2012). Moreover, we believe these differences reflect that confidence and similarity judgements are differentially affected by sources of information distinct from memory, including decision criterion influences (Jordan, 2021).

In interpreting these findings, we argue that the relationship between the three recognition approaches is nuanced. Specifically, we believe that subjective assessments of similarity precede and inform more complex judgements of confidence (Fitousi, 2024), and by extension, identity (Zwartz, 2016), in lineup-based recognition contexts. This belief aligns with theoretical accounts of similarity and confidence processing, which respectively position similarity as a relatively simple *match-based comparison process* (Kaplan & Medin, 1997; Markman & Medin, 1995) and confidence and identity as more complex *cognitive processes* that rely on match-based comparisons (Kantner & Dobbins, 2019; Fitousi, 2024). Put simply, similarity, which is functionally synonymous with match-to-memory (Levi & Jungman, 1995; Tulving, 1981; Zwartz, 2016), likely forms part of the evidence on which confidence judgements and identification decisions emerge but is not the sole contributing factor (Baranski & Petrusic, 2001; Clark, 2011). This reasoning is also consistent with signal detection theory, which posits that identification decisions result from the comparison of match-to-memory information against a decision criterion (i.e., a pre-set internal threshold for responding) and that confidence measures the distance between match-to-memory and a decision criterion (Baranski & Petrusic, 2001; Clark, 2011; Sauer et al., 2008). According to this theoretical account, neither identification nor confidence can be considered pure or direct measures of match-to-memory (Kantner & Dobbins, 2019; Turner et al., 2011); rather, they are both reliant on, and vulnerable to, a broad combination of memorial and non-memorial influences, including feelings of familiarity, deductive reasoning, decision criterion placement, administrative pressures, and individual differences (Colloff et al., 2021; Dodson & Garrett, 2021; Jordan, 2021; Steblay & Brooks, 2021).

For the reasons set out above, we believe that similarity judgements represent the most transparent reflection of match-to-memory information available to eyewitness researchers and criminal justice system stakeholders. This is because of the three approaches, only similarity obtains evidence on a continuum *and* frames this evidence in terms that are reflective of match or resemblance. Our interpretation does not suggest similarity judgements produce more accurate outcomes than identification decisions or confidence judgements; rather, that similarity judgements more accurately reflect the information available to witnesses in responding to a lineup-based recognition task.

While the idea that similarity judgements provide the most transparent reflection of match-to-memory information is neither radical nor novel (Australian Law Reform Commission [ALRC], 1985; Levi & Jungman,

1995; Navon, 1990; Thomson, 1982), it is one that has mostly failed to resonate with researchers developing alternative approaches to identification (Jordan, 2021; Zwartz, 2016). In fact, even researchers who have accepted that similarity forms the basis of identification decisions have mostly rejected the idea that it might be used as a mechanism for obtaining eyewitness evidence (e.g., Navon, 1990). Perhaps one reason for this is that there are notable concerns about the practical application and utility of approaches that try to obtain eyewitness evidence in forms other than identity (Colloff et al., 2021; Dodson & Garrett, 2021; Leippe & Wells, 1995; Steblay & Brooks, 2021).

Accordingly, in Chapter 5, we addressed the second research aim by evaluating the practical utility of confidence and similarity judgements as alternatives to identification decisions in lineup-based recognition tasks. We reported three sets of analyses that compared the discrimination accuracy (i.e., the group-level capacity of participants to distinguish between targets and replacements) and reliability (i.e., the probability that a decision or judgement made with a certain level of confidence or similarity is correct) of identification decisions, confidence judgements, and similarity judgements, and explored whether the discrepancy information, unique to confidence and similarity judgements, could enhance response accuracy.

Our first two sets of analyses revealed that confidence and similarity judgements, when collapsed into the equivalent of a single categorical response (i.e., max judgements), produced levels of response accuracy comparable to identification decisions. Specifically, estimates of discrimination and reliability did not differ across the three recognition approaches in the no-change or change conditions. However, the accuracy of identification decisions, confidence judgements, and similarity judgements all declined when target appearance changed. For example, our reliability analyses showed that the accuracy of participants' identification decisions and max judgements made with the highest level of confidence and similarity all experienced a similar, notable decline when appearance changed between encoding and retrieval. Our findings appear to challenge claims that max judgements enhance response accuracy by more precisely indexing the degree of match between a lineup member and a participant's memory of the target (Sauer et al., 2019a; Zwartz, 2016). Contrary to this proposition, our findings suggest that max confidence and similarity judgements produce a similar assessment of match-to-memory to identification decisions. Based on these findings, it may be tempting to argue that the two alternative approaches offer limited practical utility. However, we believe this argument overlooks the fact that the three recognition approaches produce comparable levels of accuracy, and that the confidence and similarity approaches provide additional information (e.g., discrepancy) that could prove valuable in applied settings.

Our final set of analyses revealed that when discrepancy information was considered, both the confidence and similarity approaches yielded meaningful information with potential practical utility. For example, the discrimination of confidence and similarity judgements generally increased with higher discrepancy. Interestingly, the discrepancy data presented a clear trend whereby discrimination for confidence and similarity judgements often exceeded discrimination for identification decisions once discrepancy thresholds reached moderate to high levels. Furthermore, while discrimination performance declined at all discrepancy thresholds when target appearance changed, discrimination still trended higher in both appearance conditions as discrepancy increased. This meant that as discrepancy thresholds reached moderate to high levels, discrimination for confidence and similarity judgements exceeded discrimination for identification decisions, irrespective of whether target appearance changed between encoding and retrieval. Therefore, our findings support recent claims that large discrepancies between one lineup member and other members of the lineup reflect strong match-to-memory signals, and thus, can be extremely informative (Brewer et al., 2012; Brewer et al., 2020; Sauer et al., 2019a; Zwartz et al., 2024).

In interpreting these findings, we believe that confidence and similarity judgements offer potential practical utility, particularly when consideration is given to the full pattern of judgements. As discussed in Chapter 5, we produced at least some evidence to suggest that confidence and similarity judgements could outperform identification decisions in terms of discrimination. The implications of this finding are important, as researchers have previously argued that alternative approaches must facilitate consistent and dramatic improvements to discrimination accuracy relative to the traditional identification approach, to be considered viable in applied settings (Colloff et al., 2021; Dodson & Garrett, 2021). While the discrepancy findings are promising, we hesitate to draw any firm conclusions regarding the practical utility of either confidence or similarity judgements due to the limitations of our research. Accordingly, we recognise the need for additional research to replicate and extend the research presented in this book. Specifically, research is needed to test the boundary conditions under which discrepancy as a variable might enhance recognition performance. This research should examine whether discrepancy can facilitate improvements in response accuracy and increase the amount of diagnostic information obtained from lineups when tested across larger, more diverse datasets and under broader experimental conditions. In addition, this research should examine whether the perceived value of discrepancy for confidence and similarity judgements is maintained when similarity increases between the target and target replacement (replacement), and different numeric and verbal response scales are utilised.

Psychological and Legal Implications

To maximise the value of eyewitness evidence and reduce the incidence of costly errors, we believe there is a need to address the main issues of identification, both psychological and legal. The main *psychological issue* of identification pertains to the fact that witnesses lack the necessary information required to reliably identify a perpetrator presented as part of a lineup, when encountered only briefly at the time of a criminal event (Levi & Jungman, 1995; Thomson, 1982). In expanding on this issue, it is important to consider that witnesses are often forced to make inferences regarding the *likely identity* of an unfamiliar perpetrator, based primarily on the visual pattern of information available at the time of encoding (i.e., during the criminal event) and retrieval (i.e., during a lineup presentation). However, this visual pattern of information is not a reliable indicator of identity, because appearances can be deceiving (Jordan et al., 2025). Our empirical findings provide a useful representation of this issue because changing target appearance between encoding and retrieval contributed to a large reduction in the accuracy of identification decisions (i.e., loss of correct target identifications). These findings not only reinforce how participants, in an experimental context, rely extensively on match-to-memory information to inform decision making; they also highlight the risks associated with presenting what appear to be subjective assessments of match between a perceptual, present representation of a person and a memorial representation of a person, in terms of identity (i.e., sameness; see Jordan et al., 2025).

An important consideration of our research is whether confidence and similarity judgements can address the main psychological issue of identification. While our research did not seek to directly answer this question, it did seek to further understand the relationship between the constructs of identification, confidence, and similarity in lineup-based recognition contexts. Consistent with our findings relating to identification, making changes to target appearance between encoding and retrieval contributed to a large reduction in the accuracy of max confidence and similarity judgements (i.e., loss of target max judgements). In addition, our Chapter 4 comparisons revealed a high degree of correspondence in participant responses made across the three recognition approaches. As discussed earlier in this chapter, these findings suggest that both confidence and similarity judgements access and rely on match-to-memory information. It could be argued, based on these findings, that both confidence and similarity judgements are susceptible to the same errors that plague identification decisions. However, the issue of identification is not that witnesses make identification errors, because memory is fallible. The issue of identification is that characterising match-to-memory, the basis of which is visual or perceptual information, as a reliable marker of identity, is artificial and misleading.

Proponents have argued that the non-categorical nature of confidence judgements removes the "all or nothing" aspect of a categorical identification (Brewer et al., 2012; Bruer et al., 2017). However, even if this argument holds, of which there is some empirical evidence to the contrary in this book (e.g., high discrepancy); it is not clear how non-categorical confidence judgements escape the main psychological issue of identification. Participants' confidence judgements may be continuous, but they are still framed in terms of identity. It is, therefore, difficult to picture in practical terms how a unique max confidence judgement made with a value of 10 (i.e., absolute certainty that the lineup member is the target) could be considered as anything other than a positive identification (Rossmo, 2021). Further, while confidence judgements clearly index match-to-memory to an extent, confidence as a psychological construct remains ambiguous (Newirth, 2021). As discussed throughout this book, confidence in recognition is generally considered to be the product of a broad combination of influences (Colloff et al., 2021; Kantner & Dobbins, 2019; Steblay & Brooks, 2021; Turner et al., 2011). It is perhaps unsurprising, then, that even some proponents have questioned whether non-categorical confidence judgements are truly immune to non-memorial decision factors (Bruer et al., 2017).

If the non-categorical nature of confidence judgements removes the "all or nothing" aspect of a categorical identification decision, then this logic remains true for similarity judgements. Unlike confidence judgements, however, which are framed in terms of identity, similarity judgements are framed in terms of resemblance. While some researchers might argue that this is a superficial distinction, it is vitally important when seeking to address the main psychological issue of identification. Consider that in practical terms, a unique max similarity judgement made with a value of 10 (i.e., highly similar to the target) can only be interpreted as a subjective assessment of the match or resemblance that exists between a participant's memory of the target and a lineup member. As such, we believe this resemblance framework better reflects the capabilities of witnesses, and the match-to-memory information on which they base identification decisions and confidence judgements. This is not to say that similarity judgements represent the only possible solution, or even the best one. In fact, we recognise that there may be some "insurmountable" practical and legal challenges associated with an approach like similarity (ALRC, 1985; Brewer & Doyle, 2021; Leippe & Wells, 1995), that in no way acts as a marker of "guilt" (Navon, 1990; Thomson, 1982). However, if the intention is to address the psychological issue of identification, researchers, and practitioners need to acknowledge that eyewitness evidence should be obtained and presented in terms that reflect what it is (i.e., similarity or match), not what we would like it to be (i.e., identity). In this regard, we believe similarity judgements are uniquely placed to address the psychological issue of identification.

The second issue of identification, and the main *legal issue*, pertains to the fact that the strength attributed to eyewitness evidence far outweighs its probative value (i.e., evidentiary or legal proof; see Wells et al., 2006). Although the focus of our research was restricted to lineup-based recognition tasks, we believe it is still worth reflecting on if, and how, the two alternative approaches examined in this book might be positioned to address this issue. Currently, eyewitness evidence is presented as a form of direct evidence (Heller, 2006); however, proponents of both confidence and similarity have assumed that if non-categorical judgements were to replace identification decisions, they would be presented as probabilistic or circumstantial evidence (Brewer & Doyle, 2021; Sauer et al., 2019a; Zwartz, 2016). Presenting eyewitness evidence in a circumstantial manner would potentially offer a more accurate representation of a witness's experience, but would also weaken its strength. This is because direct evidence directly implicates the suspect and can serve as the sole basis for a conviction, whereas circumstantial evidence does not directly implicate the suspect and therefore must be considered with other forms of evidence to secure a conviction (Heller, 2006; Sauer et al., 2019a; Zwartz et al., 2024). Historically, there has been some opposition to the idea that eyewitness evidence could assume the form of circumstantial evidence (ALRC, 1985). This opposition emerged amid concerns that eyewitness evidence could be weakened so substantially that its impact in courtrooms would become negligible (ALRC, 2006). However, we reason that if a goal of the criminal justice system is to reduce the number of wrongfully convicted innocent suspects (see Clark, 2011; Lampinen et al., 2018), then reducing the strength attributed to eyewitness evidence is desirable.

It is important to acknowledge that although proponents of non-categorical approaches have mostly assumed that judgements would take the form of circumstantial evidence, there is no guarantee that this would be the case (Simon, 2012). Brewer and Doyle (2021) touched on this subject and conceded that if confidence judgements were to become a functional component of investigatory and evidentiary practice, they would need to be converted into some "new form of evidence". We presume the same could be argued for similarity judgements, despite Zwartz's (2016) assertion that they could assume the form of "evidence of resemblance"; a type of circumstantial evidence that already exists within the Australian legal framework. Indeed, history suggests that the criminal justice system is fiercely resistant to reform (Newirth, 2021) and would fight any changes to legal doctrine that might be interpreted as beneficial for the defence (ALRC, 1985; Fisher, 2021). At the very least, we recognise that the strength alternative forms of evidence would assume in court, would likely be the subject of lengthy and intensive debate.

Before we progress, we must acknowledge that not all researchers and policymakers will share our views on the psychological and legal issues of identification. For example, many researchers believe identification decisions can be "reliable" under certain conditions (e.g., Brewin et al., 2020; Semmler et al., 2018; Wixted & Mickes, 2022). While this is a contentious position (see Berkowitz et al., 2022a, 2022b; Moore et al., 2024; Sauer et al., 2019b; Smith et al., 2021), the fact that many researchers share this belief highlights the scale of the challenge ahead for advocates of alternative approaches to lineup-based recognition. Indeed, it stands to reason that many researchers and policymakers will question the need for alternative approaches that require substantive changes to be made to public policy, the law and the criminal justice system (ALRC, 1985; Dodson & Garrett, 2021; Leippe & Wells, 1995; Newirth, 2021). We do not make this point to dismiss divergent viewpoints, or as an attempt to minimise the numerous or protracted challenges likely to face alternative approaches to lineup-based recognition. In fact, we recognise that substantial effort is still required to establish robust theoretical and practical justifications for adopting alternative approaches to lineup-based recognition. In this regard, it is vitally important that researchers evaluate novel or alternative approaches with a critical mindset and take the time to thoroughly question, challenge, and explore their potential strengths *and* weaknesses. This is especially true in the context of non-categorical alternatives like confidence and similarity judgements, which would require "enormous conceptual" and practical changes to the criminal justice system (Zwartz, 2016) and extend beyond what many researchers and policymakers might consider "reasonable or practicable" (Leippe & Wells, 1995). However, regardless of whether researchers and policymakers agree with our framing of the issues or share our optimism regarding the potential of alternative approaches, we hope that our work encourages the research community to continue reflecting on the big picture issues associated with the psychology of eyewitness identification, and in doing so, are emboldened to seek ambitious solutions.

Limitations and Future Research

Like all empirical research, the research presented in this book was subject to several limitations. For brevity, we do not reiterate limitations already addressed elsewhere in the book. Instead, we reflect on three important limitations, the second and third of which are endemic to the experimental paradigm used in this and other eyewitness research (see Jordan, 2021, Chapter 8, for complete discussion).

The first limitation, which specifically relates to our research, is that we used still photographs as encoding stimuli. We recognise that still photographs of the target, taken from a single angle, are not representative of a criminal event in real-world contexts. This is because in real-world contexts, witnesses often encode a moving perpetrator, from multiple angles, while being exposed to several additional contextual factors. We used still photographs obtained from the multi-PIE face database in the present research because it allowed us to examine the influence of naturalistic changes to target appearance. This was possible because multi-PIE includes still photographs of individuals obtained periodically over a course of six months (Gross et al., 2010). We acknowledge that presenting participants with a mock crime video at encoding would better capture the "mundane realism" associated with a criminal event (Lindsay et al., 2012). However, to the best of our knowledge, there are no openly available mock crime videos which capture naturalistic changes to target appearance. As our research indicates that changes to appearance have a large detrimental impact on recognition (Jordan, 2021; Jordan et al., 2024; Jordan et al., 2025; Thomson 1982), additional research should develop and utilise more ecologically valid encoding stimuli to better understand how these appearance changes impact witnesses in real-world contexts.

The second limitation is that the potential consequences associated with making an erroneous response in an experimental setting are not comparable to those in applied settings. In an experiment, for example, participants are aware that making an error has no real-world consequence associated with it. By comparison, in an applied setting, witnesses are aware that making an error may result in an innocent suspect being wrongfully convicted and/or allow a guilty suspect to cause more harm to society through further criminality (Amendola & Wixted, 2015). Within the constraints of the experimental paradigm, this limitation is not easily addressed. Therefore, additional research is needed at a conceptual level to investigate how to replicate at least some of the pressures felt by real-world witnesses. This may involve the development of research materials which better imitate a criminal event, while retaining existing ethical standards.

The third and final limitation relates to the general ignorance we, and other researchers, have shown for source monitoring. Recognition in experimental settings is reliant to a major extent on feelings of familiarity, the basis of which, we have argued, is a participant's subjective sense of similarity (Jordan, 2021; Jordan et al., 2025; Thomson, 1982; Thomson, 1989; Zwartz et al., 2024). In the context of a lineup-based recognition task, the familiarity of a face is directly linked to the experiment (Davies, 1989). For example, participants in an experimental setting can logically expect that if a face presented as part of a lineup is familiar (i.e., generates a strong match-to-memory signal), then this face was encountered previously as part of the experiment (Ellis, 2019). This is not the case in applied settings, where recognition is also reliant on establishing the source of familiarity (Thomson, 1986). For example, a witness in an applied setting must determine, first, that a lineup member is familiar, and, second, that the perpetrator witnessed during a criminal event was the source of this familiarity (Davies, 1989). The lack of consideration for source monitoring is particularly important in the context of non-categorical alternative approaches to recognition. This is because confidence and similarity judgements both rely on and capture perceptual or memorial information (i.e., feelings of familiarity). It is not yet clear how participants might respond using non-categorical alternatives when the familiarity associated with lineup members could be attributed to multiple, unfamiliar sources. Therefore, future research must consider how both traditional and alternative approaches (i.e., identification decisions, confidence judgements, and similarity judgements) to obtaining evidence from lineups perform when source familiarity is manipulated.

We also believe that there are several specific directions for future research that need to be addressed to ensure the continued development of alternative approaches to lineup-based recognition. For example, it is important that researchers continue to test the feasibility and viability of the two non-categorical approaches to lineup-based recognition examined in this book. As discussed throughout this chapter, both confidence and similarity judgements have potential practical utility and may be positioned to address one or both issues of identification, to varying extents. However, despite some initial promise, the full potential of non-categorical approaches to lineup-based recognition has yet to be fully realised. Therefore, eyewitness researchers should be encouraged to conduct large-scale studies that manipulate a broad variety of testing conditions, and systematically evaluate how alternative approaches to obtaining eyewitness evidence from lineups compare to the traditional identification approach, and each other. In this regard, future research should assess not only how non-categorical confidence and similarity judgements perform with respect to traditional outcome measures (i.e., target-replacement discrimination and reliability), but also how they compare with respect to novel outcome measures increasingly of interest to researchers and practitioners (e.g., rule out potential, see Smith et al., 2024; expected information gain; see Starns et al., 2023). To be optimally informative, future research in this area should direct its attention more explicitly to the features that make alternative responses distinct from identification decisions. For non-categorical approaches, this would involve avoiding the tendency to collapse multiple judgements into a single categorical response. As members of our research team and others have previously argued, collapsing non-categorical judgements into the equivalent of a categorical decision appears to wash out much of their applied benefits (Sauer et al., 2019a; Zwartz et al., 2024). Indeed, as Zwartz (2016) stated, the goal of non-categorical alternative approaches should be to produce measures of eyewitness evidence that are more informative, transparent, and distinct than identification decisions, not to "achieve identification by another method" (p. 139).

Future research should also continue to develop and explore the utility of other alternative approaches to obtaining eyewitness evidence from lineups. In this regard, researchers should be ambitious and encouraged to deviate from or iterate on the alternative approaches described in this book. For example, we welcome the recent introduction to the literature of several "hybrid" approaches to recognition, including the "rule out" (i.e., participants presented with a lineup to make a categorical identification and then provide confidence judgements for all non-selected lineup members; Ayala et al., 2022; Smith & Ayala, 2021; Smith et al., 2023); and "ranking" procedures (i.e., participants to order the lineup members based on their resemblance to an encoded target, and then make a categorical identification; Carlson et al., 2019). Hybrid approaches, as the name implies, seek to combine elements of traditional and alternative approaches to lineup-based recognition. While initial findings suggest hybrid approaches can offer valuable insights (Ayala et al., 2022; Carlson et al., 2019; Smith et al., 2024; Tuttle et al., 2025), we have some reservations about any approach that continues to frame eyewitness evidence in terms of identification, not least because it restricts their capacity to address the psychological and legal issues of identification. Thus, to better understand the full functionality of alternative approaches to lineup-based recognition, research should systematically examine how hybrid and other emerging alternatives compare to the traditional identification approach and alternative approaches described in this book. This research should not only look to assess how different approaches compare with respect to traditional and novel outcome variables but also consider how the evidence obtained using each is interpreted by triers of fact.

Finally, future research must consider how evidence obtained using alternative approaches might be used during the evidentiary stage of the criminal justice system. Understandably, to this point, research has primarily sought to establish whether alternative approaches for obtaining eyewitness evidence from lineups are theoretically relevant and empirically robust. However, the restricted focus of existing research has led to a dearth of knowledge regarding how evidence obtained using alternative approaches like confidence or similarity judgements might be presented in court or interpreted by triers of fact (Sauer et al., 2017). This gap in understanding needs to be addressed, for in its absence, it is difficult to see how a case could be made to operationalise either confidence or similarity judgements in applied settings. We believe an important consideration of this research will be to determine if patterns of judgements obtained using non-categorical approaches do enough to safeguard innocent suspects in courtroom settings. Even if we accept that judgements might assume the form of circumstantial evidence in court, it is not clear how persuasive this evidence would be. For example, we do not know how triers of fact would interpret a pattern of judgements where, say, an innocent suspect received the highest confidence or similarity judgement and was assigned a judgement of moderate-to-high value. Recently, Zwartz et al. (2024) sought to dismiss this potential vulnerability, particularly as it relates to similarity judgements, by suggesting that "using [non-categorical judgements] will not eliminate the potential for innocent persons to be rated as more [like the target] than other line-up members, but it will eliminate the aura of certainty surrounding a positive identification in such cases and minimise the likelihood of the jury being misled by it" (p. 14). However, future research needs to determine the veracity of this statement.

Summary and Final Reflections

In this chapter, we synthesised the key empirical findings reported in Chapters 4 and 5 and explored their relevance for theory and practice. We reflected on the implications of our findings for the psychological and legal issues of identification and considered how non-categorical alternative approaches to recognition might be used to address the persistent challenges associated with the traditional identification approach. Finally, we discussed key limitations that we feel must be addressed to support the continued advancement of eyewitness research and outlined important avenues for future research.

We contend that if the criminal justice system is to reduce costly evidentiary errors, such as wrongful convictions, it must ensure that procedural expectations reflect witnesses' capabilities, and that the evidentiary weight assigned to eyewitness evidence aligns with its true probative value. Based on the findings reported in this book, we argue that non-categorical confidence and similarity judgements offer, to varying degrees, promise in addressing these dual concerns. However, of the alternative approaches, we believe that similarity judgements represent the most transparent reflection of match-to-memory information available to researchers and policymakers, and as such, are best placed to address the main issues of identification. This is because only similarity judgements obtain evidence on a continuum *and* present this evidence in terms that are reflective of match. Despite our enthusiasm for the similarity approach, we recognise that this must be tempered by the realities of investigatory and evidentiary reform. Furthermore, we accept that many researchers and policymakers will have legitimate concerns about any approach to lineup-based recognition that does not provide a definitive marker of a suspect's guilt or innocence. For these reasons, we have emphasised the need for sustained empirical attention in this area.

In conclusion, it is important to reiterate that the purpose of this book was not to provide a definitive solution to the issues of identification. Indeed, we do not claim that any single approach explored in this text offers a complete solution to the challenges faced by eyewitness researchers and policymakers. Instead, we have sought to better understand and critically examine the potential of alternative non-categorical approaches to lineup-based recognition. Looking ahead, we advocate for ambition, both in how researchers conceptualise the broader issues of identification, and in their commitment to design, test, and refine innovative solutions. In this regard, we hope the work presented in this book encourages critical reflection and stimulates continued interest in the potential of alternative approaches to lineup-based recognition.

References

Amendola, K. L., & Wixted, J. T. (2015). Comparing the diagnostic accuracy of suspect identifications made by actual eyewitnesses from simultaneous and sequential lineups in a randomised field trial. *Journal of Experimental Psychology*, *11*, 263–284. http://doi.org/10.1007/s11292-014-9219-2

Australian Law Reform Commission. (1985). *Evidence: Volume 1. ALRC 26*. Retrieved from https://www.alrc.gov.au/publication/uniform-evidence-law-alrc-report-102/13-identification-evidence/background-identification-evidence-under-the-uniform-evidence-acts/

Australian Law Reform Commission. (2006). *Identification evidence*. Retrieved from www.alrc.gov.au/publications

Ayala, N. T., Smith, A. M., & Ying, R. C. (2022). The rule-out procedure: Increasing the potential for police investigators to detect suspect innocence from eyewitness lineup procedures. *Journal of Applied Research in Memory and Cognition*, *11*(4), 489–499. https://doi.org/10.1037/mac0000018

Baranski, J. V., & Petrusic, W. M. (2001). Testing architectures of the decision-confidence relation. *Canadian Journal of Experimental Psychology/Revue Canadienne de Psychologie Expérimentale*, *55*(3), 195–206. https://doi.org/10.1037/h0087366

Berkowitz, S. R., Garrett, B. L., Fenn, K. M., & Loftus, E. F. (2022b). Eyewitness confidence may not be ready for the courts: A reply to Wixted et al. *Memory*, *30*(1), 75–76. https://doi.org/10.1080/09658211.2021.1952271

Berkowitz, S. R., Garrett, B. L., Fenn, K. M., & Loftus, E. F. (2022a). Convicting with confidence? Why we should not over-rely on eyewitness confidence. *Memory*, *30*(1), 10–15. https://doi.org/10.1080/09658211.2020.1849308

Brewer, N., & Doyle, J. (2021). Changing the face of police lineups: Delivering more information from witnesses. *Journal of Applied Research in Memory and Cognition*, *10*(2), 180–195. https://doi.org/10.1016/j.jarmac.2020.12.004

Brewer, N., Weber, N., & Guerin, N. (2020). Police lineups of the future? *American Psychologist*, *75*(1), 76–91. https://doi.org/10.1037/amp0000465

Brewer, N., Weber, N., Wooton, D., & Lindsay, D. S. (2012). Identifying the bad guy in a lineup using confidence judgements under deadline pressure. *Psychological Science*, *23*(10), 1208–1214. https://doi.org/10.1177/0956797612441217

Brewin, C. R., Andrews, B., & Mickes, L. (2020). Regaining consensus on the reliability of memory. *Current Directions in Psychological Science*, *29*, 121–125. https://doi.org/10.1177/0963721419898122

Bruer, K. C., Fitzgerald, R. J., Price, H. L., & Sauer, J. D. (2017). How sure are you that this is the man you saw? Child witnesses can use confidence judgements to identify a target. *Law and Human Behaviour*, *41*(6), 541–555. https://doi.org/10.1037/lhb0000260

Carlson, C. A., Jones, A. R., Goodsell, C. A., Carlson, M. A., Weatherford, D. R., Whittington, J. E., & Lockamyier, R. F. (2019). A method for increasing discriminability and eliminating top row preference in photo arrays. *Applied Cognitive Psychology*, *33*(6), 1091–1102. https://doi.org/10.1002/acp.3551

Clark, S. E. (2011). Blackstone and the balance of eyewitness identification evidence. *Albany Law Review*, *74*(3), 1105. Retrieved from http://www.heinonline.org.ezproxy.ecu.edu.au/HOL/Page?

Colloff, M. F., Wilson, B. M., & Flowe, H. D. (2021). Legal system v. Eyewitness: The jury is still out on who is better able to reduce eyewitness error (variance). *Journal of Applied Research in Memory and Cognition*, *10*(2), 200–204. https://doi.org/10.1016/j.jarmac.2021.04.001

Davies, G. (1989). The applicability of facial memory research. In A. W. Young & H. D. Ellis (Eds.), *Handbook of research on face processing* (pp. 557–562). Elsevier.

Dodson, C. S., & Garrett, B. L. (2021). Can we get over IDs? *Journal of Applied Research in Memory and Cognition*, *10*(2), 212–214. https://doi.org/10.1016/j.jarmac.2021.03.008

Ellis, S. (2019). *Simultaneous vs sequential. Identification accuracy with previously seen innocent suspects*. [Doctoral thesis, Deakin University]. Research Online Institutional Repository. http://dro.deakin.edu.au

Fisher, R. P. (2021). On the real-world benefits and costs of assessing confidence of suspects and fillers in lineups: Commentary on Brewer and Doyle (2021). *Journal of Applied Research in Memory and Cognition*, *10*(2), 205–207. https://doi.org/10.1016/j.jarmac.2021.04.002

Fitousi, D. (2024). A signal detection-based confidence-similarity model of face matching. *Psychological Review*, *131*(3), 625–663. https://doi.org/10.1037/rev0000435

Gross, R., Matthews, I., Cohn, J., Kanade, T., & Baker, S. (2010). Multi-PIE: Proceedings of the International Conference on Automatic Face and Gesture Recognition. *IEEE International Conference on Automatic Face & Gesture Recognition*, *28*, 807–813. https://doi.org/10.1016/j.imavis.2009.08.002

Heller, J. (2006). The cognitive psychology of circumstantial evidence. *Michigan Law Review*, *105*(2), 24. Retrieved from http://www.jstor.org.ezproxy.ecu.edu.au/stable/40041577

Jordan, D. T. (2021). *Identity: A crisis of confidence? Or is it resemblance? An exploration of the different approaches by which eyewitness evidence can be obtained from lineups*. [Doctoral thesis, Edith Cowan University]. Research Online Institutional Repository. https://ro.ecu.edu.au/theses/2449

Jordan, D. T., Scott, A. J., & Thomson, D. M. (2024, July 10). Think you could pick a criminal suspect out of a lineup? If they've shaved or changed their clothes, you'd probably fail. The Conversation. Retrieved from https://theconversation.com/think-you-could-pick-a-criminal-suspect-out-of-a-lineup-if-theyve-shaved-or-changed-their-clothes-youd-probably-fail-233117

Jordan, D. T., Scott, A. J., & Thomson, D. M. (2025). Appearances can be deceiving: How naturalistic changes to target appearance impact on lineup-based decision making. *Psychology, Crime & Law*, *31*(4), 1–28. https://doi.org/10.1080/1068316X.2023.2243001

Kantner, J., Dobbins, I. (2019). Partitioning the sources of recognition confidence: The role of individual differences. *Psychonomic Bulletin & Review*, *26*, 1317–1324. https://doi.org/10.3758/s13423-019-01586-w

Kaplan, A., & Medin, D. (1997). The coincidence effect in similarity and choice. *Memory and Cognition*, *25*(4), 570–576. https://doi.org/10.3758/BF03201130

Lampinen, J. M., Smith, A. M., & Wells, G. L. (2018). Four utilities in eyewitness identification practice: Dissociations between receiver operating characteristic analysis and expected utility analysis. *Law and Human Behavior*, *43*(1), 26–44. https://doi.org/10.1037/lhb0000309

Leippe, M. R., & Wells, G. L. (1995). Should we be partial to partial identification? A commentary on the Levi-Jungman proposal. *Criminal Justice and Behaviour*, *22*(4), 373–385. https://doi.org/10.1177/0093854895022004002

Levi, A. M., & Jungman, N. (1995). The police lineup: Basic weaknesses and radical solutions. *Criminal Justice and Behaviour*, *22*(4), 347–372. https://doi.org/10.1177/0093854895022004001

Lindsay, R. C. L., Mansour, J. K., Bertrand, M. I., Kalmet, N., & Melsom, E. I. (2012). Face recognition in eyewitness memory. In A. Calder, G. Rhodes, M. Johnson, & J. Haxby (Eds.), *Oxford handbook of face perception*. Oxford University Press.

Markman, A., & Medin, D. (1995). Similarity and alignment in choice. *Organisational Behaviour and Human Decision Processes*, *63*(2), 117–130. https://doi.org/10.1006/obhd.1995.1067

Moore, K. M., Pennekamp, P., Yu, C., & Zwemer, D. U. (2024). Eyewitness confidence does not necessarily indicate identification accuracy. *Policy Insights from the Behavioral and Brain Sciences*, *11*(2), 149–155. https://doi.org/10.1177/23727322241268384

Navon, D. (1990). How critical is the accuracy of an eyewitness's memory? Another look at the issue of lineup diagnosticity. *Journal of Applied Psychology*, *75*(5), 506–510. https://doi.org/10.1037/0021-9010.75.5.506

Newirth, K. A. (2021). The change to make change: A call for a moratorium on the admissibility of eyewitness identification evidence. *Journal of Applied Research in Memory and Cognition*, *10*(2), 225–228. https://doi.org/10.1016/j.jarmac.2021.05.004

Rossmo, D. K. (2021). Delivering more information to and from lineup witnesses: Commentary on Brewer and Doyle. *Journal of Applied*

Research in Memory and Cognition, *10*(2), 196–199. https://doi.org/10.1016/j.jarmac.2021.03.004

Sauer, J. D., Brewer, N., & Weber, N. (2008). Multiple confidence estimates as indices of eyewitness memory. *Journal of Experimental Psychology*, *137*(3), 528–547. https://doi.org/10.1037/a0012712

Sauer, J. D., Weber, N., & Brewer, N. (2012). Using ecphoric confidence ratings to discriminate seen from unseen faces: The effects of retention interval and distinctiveness. *Psychonomic Bulletin and Review*, *19*, 490–498. https://doi.org/10.3758/s13423-012-0239-5

Sauer, J. D., Palmer, M. A., & Brewer, N. (2017). Mock-juror evaluations of traditional and ratings-based eyewitness identification evidence. *Law and Human Behavior*, *41*(4), 375–384. https://doi.org/10.1037/lhb0000235

Sauer, J. D., Palmer, M. A., & Brewer, N. (2019a). Eyewitness identification. In N. Brewer & A. Douglas (Eds.), *Psychological science and the law*. Guilford Press.

Sauer, J. D., Palmer, M. A., & Brewer, N. (2019b). Pitfalls in using eyewitness confidence to diagnose the accuracy of an individual identification decision. *Psychology, Public Policy, and Law*, *25*(3), 147–165. https://doi.org/10.1037/law0000203

Semmler, C., Dunn, J., Mickes, L., & Wixted, J. T. (2018). The role of estimator variables in eyewitness identification. *Journal of Experimental Psychology: Applied*, *24*(3), 400. https://doi.org/10.1037/xap0000157

Simon, D. (2012). *In doubt: The psychology of the criminal justice process*. Harvard University Press.

Smith, A. M., & Ayala, N. T. (2021). Do traditional lineups undermine the capacity for eyewitness memory to rule out innocent suspects? *Journal of Applied Research in Memory and Cognition*, *10*(2), 215–220. https://doi.org/10.1016/j.jarmac.2021.03.003

Smith, A. M., Ayala, N. T., & Ying, R. C. (2023). The rule out procedure: A signal-detection-informed approach to the collection of eyewitness identification evidence. *Psychology, Public Policy, and Law*, *29*(1), 19–31. https://doi.org/10.1037/law0000373

Smith, A. M., Smalarz, L., Ditchfield, R., & Ayala, N. T. (2021). Evaluating the claim that high confidence implies high accuracy in eyewitness identification. *Psychology, Public Policy, and Law*, *27*(4), 479–491. https://doi.org/10.1037/law0000324

Smith, A. M., Ying, R. C., Ayala, N. T., & Goldstein, A. R. (2024). The untapped potential of lineups: Using eyewitness memory to rule out innocent suspects. *Psychology, Crime & Law*, *30*(10), 1580–1590. https://doi.org/10.1080/1068316X.2023.2242998

Starns, J. J., Cohen, A. L., & Rotello, C. M. (2023). A complete method for assessing the effectiveness of eyewitness identification procedures: Expected information gain. *Psychological Review*, *130*(3), 677–719. https://doi.org/10.1037/rev0000332

Steblay, N. K., & Brooks, W. G. III. (2021). Practical concerns for investigations and courtroom: A commentary on Brewer and Doyle (2021). *Journal of Applied Research in Memory and Cognition*, *10*(2), 208–211. https://doi.org/10.1016/j.jarmac.2021.03.005

Thomson, D. M. (1982). The realities of eyewitness identification. *Australian Journal of Forensic Sciences*, *14*, 150–157. https://doi.org/10.1080/00450618209411171

Thomson, D. M. (1986). Face recognition: More than a feeling of familiarity? In H. D. Ellis, M. A. Jeeves, F. Newcombe & A. Young (Eds.), *Aspects of face processing* (pp. 391–399). Elsevier.

Thomson, D. M. (1989). *Psychological fiction in the court room: And they did not live happily ever after. Unpublished Manuscript*. Monash University.

Tulving, E. (1981). Similarity relations in recognition. *Journal of Verbal Learning and Verbal Behaviour*, *20*, 479–496. https://doi.org/10.1016/S0022-5371(81)90129-8

Turner, B., Van Zandt, T., & Brown, S. (2011). A dynamic stimulus-driven model of signal detection. *Psychological Review*, *118*(4), 583–613. http://doi.org/10.1037/a0025191

Tuttle, M. D., Starnrs, J. J., & Cohen, A. L. (2025). Protecting the innocent in eyewitness identification: An analysis of simultaneous and ranking lineups. *Journal of Memory and Language*, *140*(2), 104581. https://doi.org/10.1016/j.jml.2024.104581

Wells, G. L., Memon, A., & Penrod, S. D. (2006). Eyewitness evidence: Improving its probative value. *Psychological Science in the Public Interest*, *7*(2), 45–75. https://doi.org/10.1111/j.1529-1006.2006.00027.x

Wixted, J. T., & Mickes, L. (2022). Eyewitness memory is reliable, but the criminal justice system is not. *Memory*, *30*(1), 67–72. https://doi.org/10.1080/09658211.2021.1974485

Zwartz, M. (2016). *Identity crisis in identification evidence: Similarity judgements as an alternative to identification decisions*. [Doctoral thesis, Deakin University]. Research Online Institutional Repository. http://dro.deakin.edu.au

Zwartz, M., Thomson, D. M., & Scott, A. J. (2024). Identity crisis in eyewitness testimony: Exploring visual similarity judgements as an alternative to identification decisions. *Criminal Law Journal*, *47*(2), 93–108.

Index

Pages in *italics* refer to figures and pages in **bold** refer to tables.

Made in the USA
Las Vegas, NV
19 September 2026

412b7af7-5585-41fb-8c1f-1de699f9fcecR02